Published by
AJH Publishing
54 Brows Lane
Formby
L37 4ED

Printed by
Ribcar
56 Lower Breck Road
Tuebrook, Liverpool
L6 4BZ

Acknowledgements

I would like to take this opportunity to thank the many people who have helped me create this social history of Italian life, Liverpool's own Little Italy. Firstly my greatest appreciation goes to Ron Formby of the Scottie Press, without him this venture would not have happened, he has shown constant enthusiasm, encouragement and tireless labour throughout, a true friend.

Also thanks to Councillor Flo Clucas, Italian Consul Nunzia Bertali, Brother Ken Vance, James Dunn, Ged Fagan, Paul Sudbury, Andy Smith, Margaret Donnelly, Helen Robinson, David Charters, John Lea, Julia Carder, Tommy & Alice O'Keefe, Terry Cooke, David Stoker, Rosaria Crolla, Debbie Ryan, Gregory Brennan, Fred Dougherty, Sister Margaret-Mary, Terry Baines, Liverpool Italia, Phil Finegan of Ribcar, Liverpool Records Office and Central Library and all the Italian families who took the time to reiterate their stories and make me so welcome during our interviews. Also thank you for the many photographs that have been used to illustrate the book and the co-operation of numerous internet websites and forums. My final appreciation goes to my mother Pat D'Annunzio, my partner John Singleton and my uncle James D'Annunzio for listening to me for hours on end and always being interested, supportive and having faith in me.

Best Wishes

Debra D'Annunzio

This book is dedicated to the memory of my Irish grandmother Agnes Saunderson and my Italian grandfather Laurence D'Annunzio, their devotion to each other has been an inspiration throughout my life.

Contents

Introduction   7

Atina   9

Liverpool's Past   11

Chain Migration   16

Skilled Artisans and Community Development   21

Mosaic and Terrazzo   26

The War Years   33

Little Italy   40

Religion   45

Entertainment   52

Re-Development   56

Family Names   60

Family Stories   61

Conclusion   104

Goodbye Scottie Road   105

Introduction

There are around 250,000 Italians in Great Britain today, their community dates back over 150 years making it one of the longest established. Their achievements were founded on social and economic struggles during the 19th century. However by the 20th century the area in Liverpool they had settled in had developed into a thriving neighbourhood producing a mixture of ice cream vendors, chip shop owners, carters, musicians, boxers, and mosaic and terrazzo layers.

The port was one of the most important and industrious in the world; imported goods from every country came through the Liverpool dock system making it an extremely prosperous town. The lure of Liverpool during its halcyon era brought together many diverse cultures and social groups all seeking employment. They set up residence in different quarters of the town, to the north settled the Italian, Irish, Jewish, German and Welsh communities whilst in the southern quarter resided the Chinese and West Indians.

The heavily inhabited streets and courts became home, and was probably not what the Italians imagined their new life would be like, however they made the best of what they had and set about developing their alien surroundings into their own Little Italy.

Liverpool was known as the 'gateway' to the new world and a stopping off point en-route to America. However, by the time some Italians finally reached Liverpool, many walking the majority of the way, they found themselves financially destitute. Most therefore settled in the Gerard Street vicinity, finding work with the intention of saving enough money to continue with the journey.

The community continued to prosper throughout the 20th century, the Italians had made Liverpool their home, even present day Liverpool has a substantial Italian presence that can be attributed to the pioneering immigrants.

The fascinating relationship between Italy and Britain is continually developing and is chiefly due to the diversity of the people within the communities.

My own family (D'Annunzio) followed the chain migration pattern in 1878, which brought them to 55 Gerard Street in the heart of the Italian neighbourhood, and like many other fellow Italians they decided to stay here setting up businesses and homes. Their children grew up attending local schools and became fluent in English, however they were instilled with deep-set religious customs and life-long traditions that even today are practised in the more devout families.

By tracing the Italians from their humble beginnings to the 21st century I have compiled a social history of family life, in the form of interviews depicting life as they remember, it is therefore my objective to present a complete comprehension of the infrastructure of the Italian way of life.

The Ducale Palace, built in 1349 by Rostaino Cantelmo. The façade has three mullioned windows and contains The Noble Floor a mosaic from the 2nd century.

The oldest part of Atina sits on a hill from which the majority of the Comino Valley can be admired.

The Cathedral of Santa Maria Assunta was first built in the 11th century, the current façade is 18th century and contains frescoes by Theodoro Mancini.

Atina

Atina is a small hilltop village in the Comino Valley and part of the Lazio region of Southern Italy; it sits just north of Monte Casino and was the home of my ancestors and many of the chain migrants that came to Liverpool. The village itself has both baroque and gothic influences and although unable to verify the exact year it was founded it is believed to date back to before Rome.

The oldest part of the village stands on a hill and is veined by the river Melfa that meanders down to the valley where Aginone lies now called Villa Latina. Very little has changed of the original village, it is a fortified hamlet with an ancient *Palagic* blocked stone wall that contains a boundary stone relating to the assignation of the lands at the time of Gracchi (the Gracchi brothers tried to pass land reforms that would result in its re-distribution amongst the farmers). Within the wall several impressive buildings have stood for centuries.

The Ducale Palace was built in 1349 and contains 'The Noble Floor' a mosaic from the 2nd century.

The Convent was built in the 17th century for the Franciscan Monks; in 1871 it became the property of Atina and used as their municipal building.

The Cathedral of Santa Maria Assunta stands imposingly in the main piazza, first erected in the 11th century, with magnificent frescos painted by Theodoro Mancini in the 19th century. My great great grandfather, Michele D'Annunzio married Fortunata Mancini who was a descendant of Theodoro in the Cathedral in 1867 and all three of their children were christened there before they migrated to Liverpool a few years later.

In turbulent times Atina had many concealed tunnels and stairways, most of which still exist today, that allowed the *Atinians* to get to the outside of the village wall without detection from the enemy. One illustrious *Atinian* became the Lieutenant of Julius Caesar.

Through my extensive research, I have learned that many of the immigrants that followed the chain migration pattern from

1860 onwards and settled in Northern England and Scotland also came from a village called Picinisco, a neighbouring village of Atina. The town at 720 metres above sea level is one of the highest points in the Comino Valley.

The Romans inhabited Picinisco in the 2nd century and there is still evidence of this today in the form of two huge stones with funeral inscriptions that refer to Plancia, who were a prominent Roman family.

In Picinisco there is a castle built during the medieval period with a later addition of a central keep. The church of San Lorenzo was originally built in the 11th century but has had many additions since.

During Picinisco's German occupation in the Second World War, the Gustav Line ran through the middle of the village. The Germans used the castle's keep as an observation point and to fire upon the British Air Force. In 1944 the site took a direct hit; eight German soldiers and two civilians were killed, after the attack the German Commander withdrew the occupation of the area to the relief of the *Piciniscians*.

Like so many small villages throughout Southern Italy the loss of their people through migration has left its mark on their social development. That's not to say the villages did not progress and flourish but they remained remorseful for their general loss of friends and family members, this is evident in the overwhelming reception you experience whenever returning to the homeland as I have done on several occasions. The mere mention of my family name spurs on fond memories and stories that have been handed down through generations.

Liverpool's Past

The Romans apparently never came to Liverpool yet several Roman coins were discovered in Harrington Street and Whitechapel during the 19th century, even the original seven streets of Liverpool were laid out in the classic Roman 'H' plan and in 1855 sewer excavations in Aigburth unearthed a pavement that was allegedly Roman. Regardless of whether the Romans came here, present day Liverpool boasts numerous classic Romanesque buildings throughout the city. By the 19th century Britain had captured the world trade market and was rapidly becoming one of the richest countries in the world. The growth of Liverpool was brought about by a rise in the standard of living amongst the city's bourgeoisie; this is irrefutably evident in the grand scale of building during this period.

St Georges Hall was designed by Harvey Lonsdale Elms in 1854 and was built on the site of the Liverpool Infirmary, a competition was held to design the hall which Elms won. The building outshone most others built at that time throughout Britain and consists of a grand hall, court rooms and a concert room. Elms died seven years before its completion.

William Brown Library and Museum was designed by Thomas Allmon in 1860, the building was a replacement for the Derby Museum in Duke Street. The majority of the funding for the project came from a merchant called Sir William Brown whom the street was named after.

The Picton Reading Room was designed by Cornelius Sherlock in 1875 and modelled after the British Museum Reading Room, Sir James Picton laid the foundation stone and in 1906 the Hornby Reading Room was added by Thomas Shelmerdine.

Walker Art Gallery was designed by Cornelius Sherlock and H.H.Vale in 1877, named after its benefactor and former Mayor of Liverpool, Sir Andrew Barclay Walker, who was born in Ayrshire and lived in Gateacre.

County Sessions House was designed by F & G Holme in 1884 the pediment of which above the entrance bears the crest of Lancashire County Council and the interior includes an Italian renaissance staircase.

Over the span of 100 years, Liverpool's diverse population had increased from 78,000 in 1800 to an impressive 685,000 in 1901.

A considerable number of the population were localised just to the rear of William Brown Street, the area became renowned for its multi cultural society. It consisted of several predominant streets… Christian Street, Clare Street, Gerard Street, Grosvenor Street, Hunter Street, Lionel Street and Whale Street and within the network of the streets lay numerous court and cellar dwellings that had become a public health concern. Each court was accessed via a long, dark entry from the road and the design prohibited both natural light and air. A tap stood in the middle of the court with a toilet at one end that was used by all occupants. A cellar would measure 12 feet square and 6 feet high; the top of the doorway ran level with either the court or street outside.

Poor sanitation resulted in rat and cockroach infestations; living in these conditions was extremely harsh and consequently ended in copious numbers of deaths.

Typhoid and cholera raged amongst the inhabitants who were mostly Irish immigrants, they had arrived in Liverpool from around 1845 onwards because of the potato crop failure. This led to thousands of people leaving their homeland to make a new life for themselves in Britain and America, more than 7,000 died in just one year despite the help they received within the city. A memorial in St Luke's Church, Leece Street is dedicated to those who lost their lives during this period.

Doctor William Duncan, who became the first medical officer of health in Liverpool was employed to alleviate the situation, he ordered the cellar dwellings to be bricked up as they were unfit for human habitation. However, with the steady flow of yet more people into what was an already overcrowded area meant the cellars were illegally re-opened causing even greater misery amongst its occupants.

Pioneers such as Denison Street resident, Kitty Wilkinson rose to national notoriety for the instigation of the first washhouse. She disregarded her own safety and allowed the clothes of cholera victims to be washed and disinfected in the cellar of her home, which became the first domestic washhouse. Local children were taken in every morning, washed and fed and the ones who had been left orphaned she accepted as her own. Kitty and her husband Tom took on the role as superintendents at the first public washhouse in Upper Frederick Street in 1842 giving the locals considerable protection against future epidemics.

Improvements in housing were made alongside the court and cellar dwellings in the form of 'landing flats' such as Victoria Square, Eldon Grove and St Martin's Cottages. By the time the Gerard Street area had become home to the Italian community Liverpool was no longer recognised as the unhealthiest port in Europe as it had forty years previously. Industrious, enterprising families enhanced the standard of living within the community and occupied the once undesirable streets.

Religion played a massive role in the lives of the Italian and Irish residents, being of the same faith; the religious commonality and traditional values between both cultures were considered paramount and ensued a certain amount of harmony within the community.

Either side of Scotland Road towards the city lay two parishes, on the western side stood Holy Cross in Great Crosshall Street built in 1860, whilst on the eastern side stood St Joseph's in Grosvenor Street built in 1844. The churches dominated the area and were a force not to be reckoned with. Competition between the parishes was always healthy and the churches became the nucleus of the community. Initially Holy Cross parish was predominantly Irish, almost eighty percent of its occupants were either Irish or of Irish decent, whilst the majority of the Italians were inclined to attend the parish of St Joseph's. Religion was strictly practised at this time and many denominations prospered such as Quaker, Methodist and Baptist.

The increasing numbers of practising Catholics within the Scotland Road area resulted in the building of more churches and so by the turn of the 20th century a total of twelve had been erected. This had the knock-on effect of producing smaller communities within close proximity of the famous Road.

Scotland Road was originally constructed in the late 18th century as a turnpike road and stagecoach route to Scotland hence the name. It was with its expansion in 1803 that smaller side streets began to appear and poorly built courts and cellar dwellings gradually began to spread. The road became a lively thoroughfare embodying a cultural melting pot of Italian, Irish, Welsh, German and Polish immigrants, with distinctive shops, characteristic pubs and a truly diverse community.

The area around Scotland Road soon became densely populated some say 'a city within a city' and the sheer volume of people living in or about the road generated its reputation. The road was legendary for the amount of pubs that dominated its entirety each with their own loyal and long established customers, who saw the pub as more of a communal gathering point, offering a sense of belonging rather than just somewhere to have a drink.

By the 20th century a decision was made to clear the majority of the slum areas and replace them with municipal tenements. The 'walk-up flats' as they became known were erected on a grand scale. Gerard Gardens replaced the best part of the original Little Italy area, but the vicinity preserved much of its unique charm and character as the majority of residents were re-housed onto specific landings enabling them to remain alongside their previous neighbours. Numerous tenements were built along Scotland Road throughout the first quarter of the 20th century these included Fontenoy Gardens, Chaucer House, Lawrence Gardens, Ashfield Gardens and Woodstock Gardens to name but a few.

Scotland Road retains some remnants of its early period; St Anthony's Church was left almost on the edge of the second Mersey Tunnel. The rest of the road towards Byrom Street (once known as Townsend Lane) was not so fortunate and became a victim of the bulldozer.

William Brown Street formerly Shaws Brow became host to Liverpool's most prestigious buildings during the 19th century including a College, Museum, Library, Art Gallery and Court Room.

Left:
St George's Hall built on the site of the Liverpool Infirmary contains court rooms, a theatre and grand hall.

Below:
A 19th century view of Scotland Road. The road was reputed to have a pub on every corner. During the height of the famine thousands of Irish immigrants lived in the court and cellar dwellings in the streets that branched off the famous thoroughfare.

Below:
Eldon Grove was one of the first 'Landing Flats' to be built during the initial stages of the slum clearance in the 19th century.

Chain Migration

Garibaldi's unification of Italy was the main cause of mass migration throughout the 19th century. The standard of living in the countryside had gradually worsened making disease and starvation widespread. Food had become the biggest concern for the Italian family costing three quarters of their income and they could no longer keep up with the rising cost of living. For centuries the entire Italian peninsula had been divided into feuding states causing considerable turbulence and many poor Italians had almost no opportunity to improve their lives. The Italians living in the south suffered more adversity than the Italians who lived in the north due to their advanced level of industrialisation which resulted in less poverty, in addition much of Southern Italy's problems were attributed to its extreme shortage of fossil fuel and iron ore.

The agricultural system was antiquated and only parts of Italy were covered by the railroad system making it impossible for some farmers to sell their produce. Another cause for the migration of so many during this time was the importing of wheat and other similar products from America making the local prices drop and unemployment rise. The farmers could no longer profitably trade; there was no other alternative but to leave Italy.

For most Italians it would have been the first time outside their country and for some the first time outside their village, a troublesome period lay ahead. In order to leave their homes they first had to gather enough money for the journey, they sold all they had left and would probably have been given some funding by their parents and extended family. They said their farewells, not knowing whether they would ever return to see the people they had known all their lives, in order to travel to a strange new country where they spoke a different language and led a life that was in dire contrast to their own.

Many of the migrants got as far as Naples and other Italian cities and decided to return to their village realising this new way of life would not suit them. And many reached Liverpool and felt the same realisation only now it was too late to return and were regretful for a long time to come.

Britain became one of the largest single recipients of Italian immigrants. However, their impact was not as great as in countries like America, Argentina and Australia.

For many migrant Italians Britain, and Liverpool in particular, was a mere stopping off point enroute to America, however by the time they had reached the port sickness and insolvency had prevailed, making Liverpool a temporary residence, but for some they would stay here permanently.

The migration period can be categorised into four distinctive divisions: -
Skilled craftsmen 1800
Political expatriates 1820's
Unskilled immigrants 1850's
Travelling craftsmen 1880's

The skilled craftsmen left Italy independently and did not follow any sort of migration trend. They were mainly from Northern Italy from areas such as Coma and Lucca and all specialized in specific fields, for example the people from Coma were expert engravers and precision instrument makers, whilst the people from Lucca made intricate plaster figurines. They married English women, and it can be assumed they did not become part of any Italian community here but rather merged into British society, nevertheless they placed the foundations for future Italians.

Political expatriates found refuge in Britain because of rebellion throughout Europe during the early quarter of the 19th century. Many were dependent on British support both financially and ethically, although the more artistic of them found employment in teaching music, painting and Italian language lessons. They were staunch supporters of the unification of Italy and set about forming the 'Nationalist Movement' in Britain.

Unskilled migrants almost all of whom walked here during the middle of the 19th century, were mainly from the mountain regions of Northern Italy, they had been land workers and farmers until extreme poverty forced them to leave. They found work on a daily basis as they travelled through numerous towns in Europe and Britain.

Once here their employment was chiefly in the form of entertaining in the streets. They arrived in the spring in order to find seasonal work, with the intention of returning to Italy with enough money to ensure their family were adequately provided for during the winter months.

Travelling craftsmen or chain migrants initiated the development of the Little Italy phenomena, throughout the latter quarter of the 19th century; many of them left Italy in groups from the same village, as in the case of Liverpool's Little Italy numerous immigrants originated from Atina and Picinisco. Within the community the earliest Italians created a support group in the form of a welcoming house or Padronismo, this meant that entire families could be re-established here in Liverpool.

The system was very popular amongst the Italians, as soon as they disembarked they headed for the Little Italy area where they were given a meal called Poor Man's Cuisine, which was a traditional pasta dish consisting of olive oil, vegetables, a rustic bread roll and accompanied with a little wine. They were offered accommodation and employment in the vicinity, which was usually in the form of catering, mosaic and terrazzo laying, music and acting. They soon prospered enabling them to buy property and establish family businesses. The Italians who were furthering their journey to America were also met by familiar faces and shown some hospitality before purchasing their ticket for passage across the Atlantic on the White Star Line. A great deal has been written of the Italian male immigrant and how his determination and desires led to his achievements, but what of the strong-minded Italian women who came to Britain, a large percentage of whom were very young and bravely left their small towns and villages also.

By the latter quarter of the 19th century travelling across the Atlantic had improved immensely, larger steam-powered ships took about a week to reach America although conditions on board were still by no means luxurious. The average Italian family travelled as third class passengers so were expected to stay below decks in cramped conditions with their luggage alongside them, they would sleep in their day clothes, wash in salt water and eat meagre meals of either soup or stew which was provided throughout the journey.

By the time some of the Italian immigrants disembarked in America they had been travelling for several months and many of the older Italians were in a poor state of health, this began to concern the American government and they made it a requisite of the shipping companies to begin a process of inspection before leaving their European port. A quarantine inspector boarded the ship when it docked in New York and anyone at that point who was found to be too ill to disembark would be returned to Europe at the cost of the shipping companies. With so many Italians arriving exhausted and unwell a further course of action was undertaken by the federal government to create a permanent building for immigrants to undergo numerous assessments before being accepted into America, the building was called Ellis Island built in 1906.

Back in Liverpool the name Ellis Island put fear into most Italian families who were intending to travel across the Atlantic. Along with the returned deportees came stories of separation and chaos thus the nickname of 'Isle of Tears' became a common association with Ellis Island and probably the reason a large number of Italians remained in Liverpool.

Chain migrants most of whom left the port of Naples and crossed the Mediterranean Sea heading for the 'New World'.

Gerard Street became the heart of Liverpool's Little Italy. The Italians found lodgings with fellow Italians and made it their home.

Santangelli's ice cream parlour can be seen at the junction of Gerard Street and Bennett Street. In front of the shop there is a motorised ice cream van which became a familiar sight around the city.

A 19th century ice cream maker, the barrel would be packed with ice, salt and a separate inner barrel containing the mixture, the churning process took many hours.

Skilled Artisans and Community Development

In Liverpool the Italians maintained the traditional way of life as they would back in Italy and Italian shops and other businesses were soon commonplace. They tended to buy from other Italians ensuring the money spent was kept within the Italian community.

The Little Italy area became a complex network of integrated prospering Italian families, who had begun to build their own empires based on time-honoured Italian crafts.

The first that springs to mind is the making of ice cream; the process was identical to the practice they brought from their native land. However, the fortunate locality of the Union Cold Stores building in Williamson Square resulted in improvements in the preparation and longevity of the ice, making it possible to travel throughout the surrounding areas selling their produce.

Although numerous families in the vicinity dabbled in the production of ice cream, the Santangelli family became very prosperous. They began their ice cream enterprise from somewhat modest beginnings selling from handcarts that were pushed around neighbouring streets, however they soon advanced towards motorised vehicles and new business premises in Bennett Street, so by the 1930's they had become one of the most predominant ice cream vendors in the area.

Other families such as the Chiappes, Capaldis, Fuscos, Podestas and Valerios also had very lucrative businesses in Liverpool at the same time.

The Chiappe's chip shop on Scotland Road was a well-known stopping off point for scores of cinema goers en-route to the Gaiety. The Chiappe family branched out into supplying other vendors with their innovative production of the ice cream wafer.

The process of making ice cream during the latter part of 19th century was not an easy practice regardless of domestic or professional premises; the procedure using a hand churn was long and repetitive. The whole family would work together for long hours making ice cream in the cellars and back yards of their homes. Milk was boiled and various ingredients added, after which, the mixture was allowed to cool until the following day. Then the process of freezing would begin, a particularly demanding chore where a barrel would be crammed with ice and salt and an inner barrel containing the mixture was turned continuously until the product was finally frozen. Time being of the essence the ice cream was packed onto handcarts and tricycles and sold within the vicinity and surrounding areas and in later years with the introduction of refrigerators and motor vehicles the ice cream was taken further into other towns and seaside resorts.

Every family had their own secret recipe, and of course, every family proclaimed to make the best ice cream!

Most ice cream at the time was served around the streets in glasses called penny licks; the ice cream would be licked from the glass for the cost of a penny. This caused many problems firstly it was extremely unhygienic as many glasses were not meticulously cleaned causing the health authorities to prohibit its sale and secondly the glasses were always being broken or disappearing altogether. The solution lay in the production of paper cone containers and further advancements in the manufacture of the edible container or wafer cups became very successful.

The resourcefulness of the ice cream families meant that during the winter months the production of ice cream would cease and the hot chestnut trade would commence. For the duration of the Second World War the government placed a ban on the production of ice cream due to the richness of the ingredients. Many of the families consequently entered into other areas of catering during this period.

The Italians always had an eye for opportunity and business acumen and began to trade in an institution that was part of their neighbour's culture and not their own, deep fried fish and chips. The families that have long been fondly remembered with the trade are Chiappes, Fredianis, Fuscos, Gianellis, Podestas, Valerios and Vermiglios. All had loyal customers and the shops had their own unique décor. Some proprietors were characters behind the counter, often entertaining the customers with traditional songs and music while their supper was frying. For many Italian families this was the means to success and so during Scotland Road's halcyon era there was nothing more Italian than fish & chips.

The Gianelli family owned the legendary chip shop on Christian Street, even the famous acts at the Empire theatre could not resist the tantalizing aroma that the shop produced and staff at the theatre would be sent for the delicious treat during the intervals.

Even the destruction of the surrounding area during war-time enemy bombing didn't deter the Gianelli's with sheer resilience and determination the chip shop remained open to serve the community. It would take more than a few nights during the May Blitz in 1941 to weaken the might of the resourceful Gianelli's. Regrettably the chip shops fate lay in the hands of a scheme that would bring to a close many of the well-loved shops in the area as part of the Mersey Tunnel development in the 1960s and 1970s.

After the war the production of ice cream resumed and a prosperous period lay ahead, the return of normality within the war-torn community meant businesses were re-invented and luxury items were purchased once more. In 1948 the ice cream industry was made to comply with new food regulations and a 'dairy mix' replaced the usual milk, eggs and sugar ingredients. The 1940s and 1950s saw the ice cream industry escalate and the most-up-to-date ice cream equipment was purchased. Motorised vehicles and chimes replaced old hand carts and pristine shop interiors with room to sit and consume your purchase was commonplace.

The evolvement of the new estates such as Kirkby and Huyton together with the motorised ice cream vans meant that the rounds became very territorial amongst the vendors. Manchester endured many conflicts between old established Italians and new arrivals from Sicily resulting in vendettas which became known as the infamous ice cream wars. Soon incidents were reported all over Britain, several vans would declare ownership to the same area ending in vicious squables, fortunately this was not a great concern in Liverpool.

Sadly the industry declined and many of the familiar shops moved to seaside towns and some families sold-out to multinational companies. With hindsight if the ice cream families of Liverpool had combined their enterprises during the turbulent times the trade may still be in existence today as in the case of the Oliveri and Fabri businesses. Olivio Oliveri and Freddie Fabri married two sisters Julia and Mary Peronia from Lucca in Northern Italy, the families left their village of Viareggio and came to Britain sometime during the 1920's. The Oliveri family first went to Scotland but eventually both families settled in Birkenhead. The Fabri family had a café in Grange Road as did the Oliveri family, however it wasn't until after the Second World War whilst standing in Hamilton Square Birkenhead Olivio Oliveri saw the potential for a successful café there. Close to the busy railway station, ferry terminal and Cammell Lairds it couldn't fail. The Oliveri family forged a partnership with Ray Peers and opened the famous café selling ice cream, milky coffee and fish & chips, even today the Oliveri family are still in the catering trade.

A tradition of impeccable quality has been handed down through the generations of café and restaurant owners, although changes in taste has resulted in a more cosmopolitan menu on offer today, but rest assured somewhere on the menu there will be a recipe that is steeped in peasant history from a 19th century hilltop village.

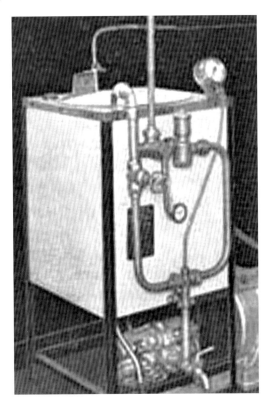

This is one of the first motorised ice cream makers.

Union Cold Stores Williamson Square.

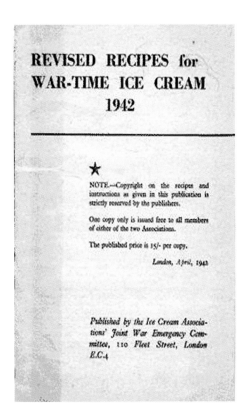

War time ice cream publication distributed amongst vendors.

Above:
This view of Richmond Row shows an
ice cream cart and a young man
enjoying a 'Penny Lick'.

Above:
Johnny and Frankie Gianelli.
This photograph was taken towards the end of
their career in their chip shop on Christian Street.

Mosaic and Terrazzo

It can be assumed that the area around Gerard Street became home to so many Italians during the middle of the 19th century because of its locality to Liverpool's most prestigious street, William Brown Street.

Liverpool was undergoing an unprecedented expansion; Shaws Brow had at one time been a thriving area dedicated to the pottery industry. However, by the mid 19th century the industry was declining and a mass clearance of the area was underway.

The buildings that replaced the old windmills and limekilns became Liverpool's finest examples of Italian and Greek classical architecture. The buildings were adorned with travertine wall cladding, the floors were inlaid with intricate mosaic tiles and the great domes were decorated with fantastic frescos, glass and plasterwork. The finest marble was imported from Italy and only the best craftsmen were hired to carry out the work.

One of the most prominent firms at the time dealing in mosaic and terrazzo was Diespeker based in Liverpool and employed most of the Italian craftsmen from the Little Italy area.

When creating a floor depending on the size there were two methods used, the first would be utilised in small areas and was called the direct method. The process involved placing individual tiles onto the surface where a picture immediately began to unfold and mistakes were easily rectified as the work progressed. The major disadvantage with the direct method was the artists spent long periods in cramped conditions with constant cuts and grazes to the hands and knees. The indirect method was often used for large projects with symmetrical and repetitive designs. The pieces were created off site, then transported and reconstructed within the building rather like a huge jigsaw.

The work was difficult and took great skill and patience; the art of mosaic laying was often handed down from father to son along with several well-kept secrets. The final procedure was the polishing, this in itself was a great skill, and the floor would take on a glass like surface and gave the illusion of an incredible masterpiece.

Above:
A mosaic in Croxteth Hall using the
'direct method' within the small confines
of a bathroom.

Left:
Marble inlay has been used to create a
symmetric pattern at Byrom Technical
College, William Brown Street.

The magnificent floor at the Port of Liverpool building.
Below is the signature of the craftsman Santini.

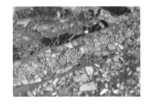

Modern day mosaic,
Debbie Ryan's Super Lamb Banana.

Above:
Here we have another fine example of Italian craftsmanship in Cooke Street.

Right:
Two second century mosaics that adorn the floor of the Ducale Palace in Atina.
The Roman soldiers are called Sannita and Querriero.

Here we have the impressive mosaics that adorn the Judge's chambers at the County Sessions House in William Brown Street. The walls are cladded with both marble and travertine stone.

Here are two examples of intricate mosaics that can be found at Sudley House, Aigburth once home to the shipping merchant George Holt.

Above:
The Philharmonic Pub has extensive mosaic and
terrazzo throughout.

Left and Right:
The Liver Building lobby has marble wall and
floor cladding.

The practice of mosaic laying was created several hundred years ago when Venetians realized a use for the left-over pieces of marble tiles and the trend soon caught on. The uneven surfaces were rubbed with 'hand-stones' until they were smooth, this process was called galera. The first craftsmen who brought this to Britain were called Friulani in the late 18th century.

Advancements in the polishing procedure with the use of machine-driven grinding equipment led to a finer finish and further introductions of the rotating carborundum stones gave the finish we have today. Mosaic flooring was used extensively in the most high-status buildings such as the buildings in Liverpool's William Brown Street, it was used to show a person's wealth, and the more vibrant the mosaic meant the more affluent the person was. This is evident in Sudley House, Mossley Hill Road in Aigburth, owned by George Holt who was a partner in the shipping firm Lamport & Holt. When the family bought the house in 1883 several alterations took place, a mosaic veranda, a conservatory with mosaic floor and mosaic vestibule were added to the house all with extensive use of expensive coloured tiles.

Liverpool's finest example of mosaic work can be found in the County Sessions House in William Brown Street, the flooring is exquisite, depicting the Rose of Lancashire. Unfortunately the building is utilized by Liverpool National Museums as offices therefore the general public can no longer appreciate its splendour.

The War Years

In 1935 an organisation called Direzione Didattica or Education Directorate began holding Italian lessons for the children of Italian immigrants living in the Little Italy area. The classes were held during the evening three times per week at Bishop Goss School with the reward of a holiday in Italy to students who showed the most potential. The Italian School was a great success partly due to the distribution of food and clothing to the more disadvantaged pupils by the organisation. However, the classes were short lived as rumours began spreading around the neighbourhood that the school was allegedly a cover up scheme to convert the local's children into adult fascists.

1939 saw the threat of war looming and so masses of young Liverpool men voluntarily enlisted to fight for 'King and Country'. Many of the men were of Italian descent (my grandfather, Laurence D'Annunzio was amongst the first to enlist in the Royal Navy). Liverpool began preparing for war, gas masks, identity cards and ration books were issued, air raid shelters were erected in the neighbourhood and the children were being evacuated, this created public unease. Rationing of food took effect in March 1940 and was already in short supply, huge queues began to appear outside shops hours before they opened in the hope of getting some fresh provisions.

Tensions were growing within the city particularly due to the amount of support Italy was already giving to Germany so early on in the war, things could only get worse.

In June of 1940, Mussolini declared allegiance with Germany making Italy an adversary of Britain; this led to a sudden shift in attitude towards the Italians and fear developed in Little Italy. The majority of residents in the community did not feel any different towards their Italian neighbours as they were aware of the young Italian men who were already fighting in the war and how some of the older Italians had fought in the First World War. Nevertheless, there were reports of gang protests around the city, Italian run businesses were set on fire, windows smashed and sickening threats scrawled on the walls. Some long family-run businesses were lost all together when they were taken-over by a government department called the Custodian of Enemy Property. Children faced hurtful taunts and abuse at school, they were told by other children their fathers and brothers would be taken to Prisoner Of War camps and they would never see them again.

The Italians were now considered the enemy by some people resulting in a number of Italians taking great pains to de-Italianise themselves by attempting to blend in and anglicise their name in order to survive their plight. A whole generation of Anglo-Italians learned to endure the unjust and hostile acts that were bestowed upon them through no fault of their own and for a considerable time to come.

The government began restricting the movements of Italian families and the Prime Minister, Winston Churchill stated all Italian Nationals residing in Britain should be "rounded up". Before Italy's involvement in the war the government had not attempted to sort out the fascists from the non-fascists but alternatively worked from a list compiled by military intelligence of over 1,500 Italian civilians living in Britain who were considered dangerous characters and, who were to be arrested immediately in the event of Italy declaring war on Britain.

In Liverpool the local Police at Rose Hill Station were instructed to visit every Italian home in the Little Italy area and take all male and some female occupants regardless of age for questioning. The night of the internment was a terrifying ordeal and one the Italian families would never forget; fathers and sons were arrested while their families looked on wondering if they would ever see them alive again. They were first taken to the local North Western Hotel in Lime Street, once there they were questioned about their involvement in the war. They were then transferred to an internment camp or collection point, one such camp was a housing estate that was still in the process of being built called Woolfall Heath in Huyton. Even at this point it was believed the authorities were already aware that the Italians who they were questioning were not dangerous fascists but harmless civilians. The men and women were separated; they were refused newspapers or to listen to the radio and receive or send letters, so were unaware of the fate of the rest of their family.

The non-threatening Italians were released whilst the ones thought to be active fascists were deported, some went to the Isle of Man whilst the remainder awaited deportation to Canada. On the 2nd of July 1940 the SS Arandora Star, originally a passenger ship built at Cammell Lairds in 1927, left Liverpool for St Johns Canada with 1299 Italian internees and German Prisoners Of War onboard. At two minutes before eight o'clock in the morning the unescorted ship was hit by a torpedo on her starboard side, from a German U-boat under the command of Günther Prien, off the coast of Donegal Ireland and sank within thirty minutes. 470 Italians lost their lives, the 586 survivors were rescued by the HMCS St Laurent and taken to Greenock in Scotland. The German POW's had been kept on the top deck whilst the Italians had been kept below in the cabins, with little chance of escape through the maze of unfamiliar corridors that had been plunged into total darkness, their chance of survival was nil. Even if they had been fortunate enough to escape to the top deck the insufficient number of lifeboats and barbed wire that flanked parts of the ship made it impossible for countless internees to survive.

The men, whose average age was over fifty, were civilians that had made their homes in Britain, had worked and created businesses here since the late 19th century, what sort of threat did they pose to national security. Survivors of the Arandora Star told how the older men from the mountain regions of Italy could not swim as they had not had any connection with the sea, so they just stood on the decks and awaited their fate.

There was an immediate investigation by the War Office into the tragic incident and at one point they considered abandoning the deportation of the survivors, who were still being sheltered in a disused factory in Greenock. Regardless of the horrifying nightmare of events onboard the Arandora Star, the Italian internees were once again put through the anguish of travelling by sea to their internment camp in Canada and whilst en-route they were again torpedoed, however this time there was no loss of life.

The families of those who lost their lives onboard the Arandora Star have never received a formal apology from the British government and the families whose businesses and personal items that had been confiscated during the war never received any compensation for the distress that they endured. Most of the families who suffered such treatment had sons fighting in the British Armed Forces, however this detail was insignificant to the British government and they continued with the deportation scheme of Italians throughout the war.

One of the longest campaigns of the war was the Battle Of The Atlantic and Liverpool's strategic location meant it became the main port for the importation of fuel, food and raw materials. This also made Liverpool the most bombed city outside London. Over 2000 merchant ships were sunk throughout the Second World War the majority of which were Liverpool bound. Most of the dock's factories and warehouses bore the brunt of the air raids with over half of the actual dock system being put out of action.

During the May Blitz of 1941 that lasted seven days, Liverpool suffered almost total devastation, Lord Street was literally unrecognisable, other buildings that were extensively damaged were the Customs House, Central Library, Lewis's and the Post Office in Victoria Street to name but a few.

On the third night of the bombing, a cargo ship called the SS Malakand, carrying tons of high explosives, was berthed at the Huskisson Dock, the ship caught fire during the air raid and exploded sending debris for miles and causing substantial damage to the overhead railway. The entire area suffered a vast amount of damage and clearing up the debris and carnage took both civilians and troops many weeks.

Nevertheless the people of Liverpool were unbeatable, every morning they came out of the shelters weary from yet another sleepless night but still carried on with their daily routine constantly re-building what had been destroyed the night before. One night during an horrendous air raid Gianelli's chip shop was almost totally destroyed by a bomb that landed in Christian Street, the shop front was ruined but with sheer determination the family had the chip shop up and running and serving the community the next day.

On the 8th of May 1945 a message was broadcasted to the nation by the Prime Minister Winston Churchill, stating a ceasefire had been signed at 02:41 yesterday and declared 'Victory in Europe'. Everyone celebrated and there were street parties all over Britain.

St Luke's Church on Leece Street was never re-built after it suffered a direct hit; only the outer walls and tower remain, it acts as a memorial to the 1,714 lives that were lost during the infamous week of the May Blitz and became known as 'the bombed-out church'.

In memory of Antonio D'Annunzio born in Atina and perished onboard The Arandora Star aged thirty-five.

Below:
Here is a scene that parents must have dreaded, their beloved children being evacuated at the beginning of the Second World War.

Here we have a group of internee's as you can see some of the men are of pension age.

Left: The cruise liner 'The Arandora Star'. It was built at Cammell Lairds in 1927 and became a Prisoner of War and internee ship during the Second World War. She was sunk off the coast of Ireland in 1941 by a German U-boat. 470 Italian internees en-route to Canada were drowned.

Below: The grand ballroom.

Below:
The newly-built housing estate Woolfall Heath in Huyton.
The estate became a temporary holding camp for many Italian internees whilst they awaited deportation

Above:
The internment camp at Peel on the Isle of Man.

Below:
Total devastation of
Holy Cross Church.

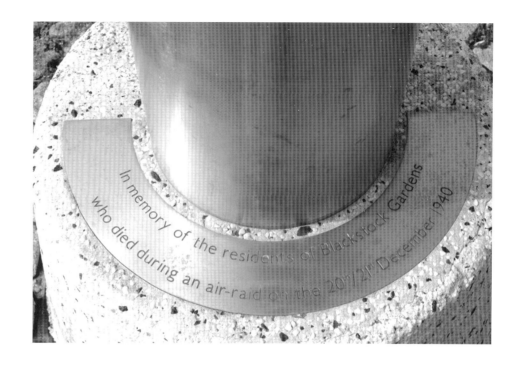

In memory of the residents of Blackstock Gardens who died during an air-raid on the 20th/21st December 1940

Above:
The monument that stands close to where an air raid shelter in the centre of Blackstock Gardens, Vauxhall (pictured right) was totally wiped out killing nearly all of its occupants.

Little Italy

The Little Italy area of Liverpool was located at the top end of Scotland Road towards the city centre. The principal roads of the vicinity were Christian Street, Circus Street, Gerard Street, Grosvenor Street, Hunter Street and Lionel Street with many smaller streets branching off. It has been written on several occasions that the area was one of the most squalid in the city; nevertheless it was home to many families who did not see it in the same light. To them it was a warm, friendly, safe environment where children played in the streets, they attended local churches and schools, and the families worked together creating lucrative businesses and developing a community that depended on individual participation in order to survive as a whole, this was their Little Italy.

The fascinating history of the area began in the 18th century. Gibson's Folly was a strange tower that stood at the junction of Islington and Christian Street, the purpose of which was unknown. Philip Christian whom the street was named after demolished the tower and used it as material for his house, which became the first house to be built on Christian Street in 1780.

Circus Street was aptly named, as the Olympic Circus Adelphi Theatre was built there in 1795. Later in 1840, it became the Adelphi Theatre Tavern and for a short spell it was used as the local boxing venue. In 1912 the building was converted into the Adelphi Picture Palace until it was demolished and rebuilt as the Adelphi Cinema, sadly it was totally destroyed by enemy action during the Second World War.

Running parallel to Circus Street was Gerard Street; it was named after the chief magistrate and leading physician Doctor James Gerard, who owned a substantial amount of land in the area. In 1796 The Quaker's Meeting House which consisted of a small church and cemetery, was built in Gerard Street, later it became The Quaker's Friend's Meeting House.

Hunter Street was one of the more wider streets in the area and named after Rowland Hunter who owned a large house there.

If it were possible to physically return to the Little Italy of the 19th century and walk within the confines of its streets the ambience would be incredible. Music from barrel organs in the streets, wonderful aromas of meals being prepared and sold in the cook houses, the sound of caged birds joyfully singing, hand carts selling ice cream in the summer and fitted with a brazier for chestnuts in the winter being pushed through the neighbourhood and the hustle of people going about their daily routines.

The average Italian home nearly always consisted of grandparents, uncles and aunts, however, some families had left their parents back in Italy and had no close relatives in Liverpool so chose fellow immigrants from their Italian village (paesano) as part of their extended family. The Italians would regularly gather to partake in the customs and traditions they grew up with; it also alleviated the loneliness and made life in a strange environment bearable. The nonnos (grandfathers) and nonnas (grandmothers) were the storytellers who would recount the tales from their childhood back in Italy to a captivated audience of grandchildren.

Each region of Italy had its own unique method of preparing for traditional feast days and religious celebrations; and in Little Italy competition amongst the Italian women was fierce. They sought out butchers who would supply the very best pork for making sausages and lamb for roasting, they would even send for grapes from Italy and make their own wine. Highly guarded secret recipes were handed down through the generations of mothers and daughters, one particular traditional recipe was 'The Feast of Seven Fishes', which contains no meat and only served at Christmas time. The preparation starts with the Novena eight days before Christmas and lasts until the Epiphany; a twenty-four hour fast was required the day before Christmas Eve after which a grand meal consisting of fish, spaghetti, vegetables and a traditional Italian dessert was served. After the feast 'The Urn of Fate' would be presented at the table, which was an ornate bowl full of wrapped Christmas gifts that was passed around the gathered family until it was empty.

Every culture has superstitions that are usually founded from religious tradition. Italians overall are immensely superstitious people, with many customs being transferred by memory from the older generations. Here are some of the more familiar ... many Italian marriages are avoided in the month of August; it was thought to invite bad luck and sickness to both bride and groom. Another quirky custom called for the groom to have a piece of iron in his pocket in order to ward off the 'evil eye' or maloccio, a similar tradition I still use today is to hang a red chilli or 'il corno' from my key-ring which averts envy. Traditionally back in Italy the parents of the bride and groom arranged the weddings, which also included choosing a potential partner, however as the Italians became more anglicised the wedding arrangements were relaxed and mixed marriages began to happen.

Italian weddings and celebrations always consisted of 'The Dance of the Tarantella' its origins date back to Southern Italy during the Middle Ages. It is a frenzied dance accompanied by guitars, mandolins and tambourines and is considered a mixture of gracefulness and passionate innuendo.

Keeping with the religious theme if an Italian physically bumped into a nun, they would immediately touch iron to protect themselves, as nuns were believed to be surrounded by bad luck.

Some Italian superstitions may border on the bizarre, but it was what made the Italians different from their fellow neighbours in Little Italy. Many of the old customs have died out with passing generations nevertheless I am sure there are simple things even non Italians do today without giving a second thought as to why they do them, for example throwing salt over the shoulder or the first footers on New Years Eve holding a piece of coal. They are all customs that have been passed down through families with their true meanings probably being altered with each transient generation.

Post war trends in Britain were centred on the film industry, popular songs and fashion, with all three being directly attributed to Italy.

The films which emphasized all things Italian were a huge hit, these included Roman Holiday, Three Coins in a Fountain and It started in Naples, and popular songs such as Mario Lanza's 'Arriverderci Roma' and Dean Martin's 'That's Amore' were amongst the most sought after.

However, the most outstanding Italian exports were the fashion icons that came in the shapely form of Gina Lollobrigida and Sophia Loren. The voluptuous sirens would have definitely inspired the women of Liverpool into wearing figure hugging clothes and creating short dark hairstyles. Whilst the men wore well-tailored Italian silk suits.

The cinema-going public could not get enough of 'La dolce vita', living the sweet life, during this jubilant period either being Italian or just living in Little Italy could not have been more popular.

The Italian lifestyle was immensely desirable to a generation just starting to enjoy a prosperous economy after years of rationing and always going without.

Lionel Street.

Howgates shop.

Clare Street.

Hunter Street.

Holly Street.

Circus Street.

Comus Street.

Religion

Religion has always been an expression of unity among people sharing the same faith, its role helped to integrate the different cultures that were living alongside one another. It also encouraged traditional rituals such as certain meals being eaten on specific days of the week and played a huge part in the lives of the Italian and Irish immigrants of Liverpool.

Several parishes were dotted along the world famous Scotland Road. St Anthonys, St Sylvesters, St Bridgets, St Marys Highfield Street and a little further on were St Francis Xaviers and St Mary of the Angels parishes, however the two that dominated the Little Italy area the most were the parishes of St Josephs and Holy Cross with Scotland Road running like an artery straight through them. Starting with St Josephs, which stood on the site of the former All Saint's Church, in 1845 was re-named but not formerly opened as St Josephs until St Patricks Day in 1848. The church became the nucleus of the neighbourhood for both Italian and Irish residents, having hundreds of parishioners and several priests Father Green, Father Montgomery, Father Tobin, Father Furlong and Father Pownall, to name but a few. This was also the height of the Irish famine and Italian chain migration keeping the priests occupied at all times.

In 1856 Bishop Alexander Goss then Bishop of Liverpool was accredited with the instigation of new Catholic churches and schools being built in Liverpool at the time, one of which was erected in Rose Place next door to St Joseph's Church and called Bishop Goss School in honour of its benefactor.

The church was host to magnificent outdoor processions that passed through the streets of the neighbourhood that had been beautifully decorated with buntings and flowers hanging from houses, the preparation of which had begun many months previously. Children were dressed immaculately; the girls strewed blessed rose petals from handcrafted baskets and proud parents watched along the roadside some even taking part carrying statues. The Priests would be dressed in vestments of vivid colours and the children in the procession would meander through the same streets their parents and grandparents had done years before, singing favourite hymns and indulging in the attention that was bestowed upon them.

Holy Cross Church was built within close proximity to where St Patrick's Cross once stood. The cross marked the spot where St Patrick allegedly preached on his way to Ireland.

In the 1840s a huge arrival of desperate Irish immigrants disembarked in Liverpool. Fleeing their own country they sought sanctuary here and settled in and around the Holy Cross area. In 1849, it was recognized that a church was required to lessen the impact on what was an already crowded St Josephs and in 1860 Holy Cross was finally opened. Designed by Edward Pugin and under the command of the Missionary Oblates of Mary Immaculate. The Missionaries tended the fever-ridden famine victims of the area, and preached the gospel to the poor, with total disregard for their own health, they entered the streets and courts of the area and cared for the parishioners who had contracted typhus and cholera.

The church embodied the spirit of the community, represented age-old traditions and beliefs, and was the epitome of hope for its congregation. The church symbolised the character of the hard-working Italian and Irish immigrants of its parish, it recognised who they were and what they aspired to be.

During the Christmas air raids of 1940, the magnificent church was one of the victims of incendiary bombing. On the 21st of December the church took a direct hit and burst into flames on impact, and although the priests, parishioners and firemen fought throughout the ongoing air raid to save their beloved church, the fire took hold and left the building completely gutted. The community were in total disbelief when they saw the tangled mess in the cold light of day. The altar and altar rail were barely visible amongst the carnage, earlier that evening the parishioners had gathered and knelt at that same altar rail and prayed for the safe return of their family members who were fighting overseas and now they were fighting for their own lives. It wasn't until 1954 that the parishioners could take mass at Holy Cross again when the newly built church was finally opened.

After the war the unsightly air raid shelter that had been built in the garden area of Fontenoy Gardens was put to good use during the summer months when many religious processions took place. The imaginative parishioners of Holy Cross transformed the shelter into a beautiful altar where the crowning of the statue took place. Frank Gianelli and numerous other men of the parish constructed the altar several times a year.

The women would then meticulously attach each handcrafted flower individually, with the diligence of the Irish and the artistic flare of the Italians the result was second to none.

Fontenoy Gardens would be full to the brim with residents and relatives looking down from the landings and people from surrounding parishes gathering below in the gardens. The procession would make its way through the streets accompanied by a band and singing well-rehearsed hymns, finally entering the gardens via the archway where the penultimate crowning took place at the improvised altar.

Not all parishes were fortunate enough to have an existing air raid shelter, one such parish was St Bridgets. The same night Holy Cross was destroyed Blackstock Garden's air raid shelter was bombed by enemy action, entire families lost their lives such as the Bellis and the Clarke families who both lived in the tenement flats. My own family lived in Blackstock Gardens and my grandmother often spoke of the pitiful sight of her friend, Katie Gregory (nee Clarke) surrounded by four coffins in her parents flat in Blackstock Street. My grandmother and her three children had been living in a small town in Scotland at the time but had come home when they heard the devastating news. My grandmother was concerned for the safety of her own parents as they often took refuge in the ill-fated shelter but on that tragic night they had decided to hide in the cupboard where the coal was kept and survived the dreadful raid. In memory of those who lost their lives, St Bridget's held a special procession in June every year, as in other processions the children would walk through the decorated streets, however the culmination of the June event took place at the site where so many were killed, a mass was heard and the deceased of the parish were remembered in the service, the priest then blessed the ground.

Religion has always offered comfort and solace to the immigrants of Liverpool regardless of their origins or faith. The social aspect of religion brought together many different cultural elements and strengthened their alliance and identities as with the Italian and Irish communities. The church became a social point and the hub of communal life, it was a place for the younger people to meet and form relationships outside their own culture, which resulted in a large number of Irish/Italian marriages.

The altar at St Mary of the Angels
Fox Street.
Its benefactor White Star Shipping
Line heiress, Amy Elizabeth Imrie
adorned the interior of the church
with the finest marble and altar
painting based on an original
in Perugino.

Philip Neri Church, Catharine Street.

The parish of St Josephs

View of Bishop Goss School and pupils with their teachers

A house in Christian Street decorated for one of the many religious processions that took place through the streets of Little Italy.

The parish of Holy Cross

The parish of St Bridget

St Bridget's held a special procession in June in remembrance of those who perished in the Blackstock Garden's air raid shelter.

Entertainment

The Italians were renowned for their artistic aptitude; and many of them were accomplished musicians. Little Italy was legendary for its street entertainers, primarily the barrel organs or hurdy gurdys, as they were more commonly known. They were often hired for a small fee and taken into the city's streets, occasionally accompanied by small dancing monkeys. Some families created lucrative businesses by manufacturing the organs and then hiring them out, some organs were unique and required intricate detailed art-work that had been passed down through generations from their native Italy.

The accordion or piano key box was another choice of entertainment amongst the Italians, they were much easier to transport than the barrel organs and were very popular with the theatre going public who would be entertained in the queue whilst waiting outside.

A well-known musical family in the neighbourhood were the Ventres, Anselmo Ventre was a talented harpist and his wife, Madalena Granelli played the mandolin. They had eleven children all of whom inherited their parent's talent and could either sing or play various instruments.

The family were familiar faces at celebrations and gatherings in the Holy Cross area helping to generate support for the re-building of the church after the war. Anselmo performed at local Masonic functions and played the harp as part of a group onboard the Mersey Ferry Cruises. Another member of the family, Tony Ventre went on to become a professional singer and sang at many top venues throughout the 1950's.

Tony Judge, whose mother was Madalena (Maud) Ventre has kept the family tradition going with his magnificent mandolin playing, he is part of a well-known group called The Wirral Mandoliers.

Public houses were the familiar haunt for the musicians where they were prepared to do a turn and in some cases be paid in beer. The street musicians were also a welcomed sight in the tenements and would often perform in the gardens, residents would congregate on the landings to listen and throw money to the entertainer below.

Another favourite form of entertainment in Little Italy was boxing and many local school boys from the area showed great promise, one of the best known was Dominic (Dom) Volante born 1905, son of Maria Grazia D'Annunzio and Vincenzo Volante, who were both born in Atina, Italy.

Dom showed huge potential in boxing, even starting up a local boxing club along with other fellow enthusiasts in the area.

During his boxing career, Dom became contender for the British Lightweight Championship and the Lonsdale Belt. In 1930, he went on to tour America and was a great success. New York during the 1930's was like home from home for Dom, with a large Italian community and a regular influx of Liverpudlian Merchant Seamen he was never short of supporters.

By 1936, Dom accepted that his boxing career had ended, with a persistent eye injury thwarting any further contests he became a gym instructor onboard the Cunard Passenger Liners, coaching many affluent people whilst they cruised the Atlantic.

Although Dom had a hard man reputation, outside the boxing ring he took on quite a different persona. He was a quietly spoken man with firm family values, a devout catholic and teetotal, he had a strong sense of community and was immensely proud of his Italian heritage.

Dominic Volante died in December 1982 at the age of 77 after a short illness, his death brought to an end an outstanding career. He was highly respected by all who had been given the pleasure of knowing him, this was clearly evident in the attendance at his funeral where mourners lined the streets.

He often reminisced about his childhood and growing up in Little Italy with fond memories, Dom was undoubtedly Liverpool's most famous boxing prodigy.

Filipo D'Annunzio proudly stands with his accordion, a favourite instrument amongst the street entertainers.

A hurdy-gurdy or barrel organ.

A piano key box.

Above:
Dom Volante pictured centre, his boxing career spanned over fourteen years and he was a respected man both inside and outside of the ring.

Above right:
Dom pictured with Everton Footballer Dixie Dean.

Right:
Dominic Valerio.

Re-Development

The old property in the Little Italy area which was considered slum by the City Planning Department was being demolished in a mass clearance project as part of the city's Homes for the Workers scheme throughout the 1930s. The replacements were sheer luxury in the form of tenement gardens. The contemporary flats housed indoor toilets, bathrooms, electricity, gas and safe areas for children to play.

City Architect, Lancelot Keay was principally in charge of the grand clearance from 1925, during his career of a mere twenty or so years he implemented the building of more than 35,000 homes across the city, one such development was Gerard Gardens.

On the 21st of June 1935 Sir Kingsley Wood, then Minister of Health, laid the foundation stone for Gerard Gardens and building work was soon in progress.

The residents still living in the old neighbourhood were hesitant about the grand plans at first. They had lived alongside each other for many years, for some of the older residents it was their only family home since leaving Italy. Their children had been born in upstairs bedrooms and had grown up playing in the streets outside, domestic businesses had been established from cellars and backyards and numerous shops would be demolished as part of the clearance. However, the buildings were quite literally falling down and the realisation of this brought about a shift in attitude in favour of the re-development.

By 1937, Gerard Gardens and Gerard Crescent had been completed but much of the old area towards Christian Street still remained. The Quaker's Friend's Meeting House that consisted of a small church and cemetery hindered development of an additional arch and several more flats to Gerard Crescent. The third stage was finally completed in 1939 with the appendage of Cartwright, Downe Lionel and Thurlow House. By 1942 the initial project had been achieved and the main entrance to Gerard Gardens was aptly decorated by two figures made from Portland stone 'The Builder and The Architect' sculptured by Herbert Tyson Smith and commissioned by Lancelot Keay, who in 1947 received a knighthood for his contribution to public housing.

Gerard Gardens soon became home to its new residents and many extended families were scattered within the complex.

Gerard Gardens developed the previous neighbourhood into a new vibrant society; the landings took on the role of the former streets and the unique arrangement of the actual buildings created a fort like environment.

By the 1950s, plans for further extensive re-development of the area was taking place, new roads and flyovers linking Islington to both Tithebarn Street and Dale Street would desecrate what was left of the old neighbourhood. By the 1960s the roads, flyovers and walkways were in place and already causing anguish to the locals especially around Byrom Street were they resembled a mini Spaghetti Junction. The residents of Gerard Gardens felt isolated, although literally on the doorstep of the city centre, the segregation of the roads restricted their movements. The flyovers were far closer than had been anticipated and in some cases ran just outside the verandas and windows of the tenements.

Throughout the 1960s and 1970s the Little Italy neighbourhood and surrounding areas became victim to the Mersey Tunnel development; people were relocated in towns lying on the periphery of Liverpool and they hardly ever returned on a regular basis. The majority of Scotland Road fell prey to the grand plans and what was not demolished lay empty and derelict.

The 1980s drew Gerard Gardens ever closer to the bulldozer and regardless of numerous demonstrations by residents 1986 saw the initial stages of demolition get underway. Within half a century, most of the city's tenements had gone from being luxurious homes to decaying hostile environments.

The area today is in dire contrast to the Little Italy of the 19th century, during the 1980s and 1990s quality homes were built on the site of Gerard Gardens for the former residents and several Italian families still remain. However the true meaning of the old community has been lost forever, the corner shops, chip shops, ice cream parlours, cinemas, pubs and churches are long gone, with individualism taking over traditionalism in the 21st century.

Much of the older property was demolished to make way for the new tenements.

The newly built Gerard Gardens.

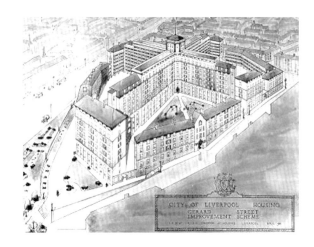

Original design of Gerard Gardens.

Comus Street today.

The bulldozers move in, making way for the Mersey Tunnel

*The Builder
which once adorned
the wall of
Gerard Gardens.*

Family Names

Arcari	Ferri	Podesta
Albertini	Franchetti	Riccio
Baccino	Frediani	Riozzi
Bartolomei	Fusco	Rocca
Boggiano	Gianelli	Russiano
Bonneretti/Boner	Granelli/Grannell	Sabatini
Bonna/Boni/Bonne	Guzzoni	Sanguinetti
Bordessa	Iello	Santangelli
Capaldi	Imundi	Sartorri
Cappella	Innelli	Silvano
Chiape	Marcari	Sinagoea
Cogliolo	Marengo	Tambourini
Colletta	Minchelli	Tremarco
Conelli	Miolla	Valerio
D'Annunzio	Minghella	Varcelli
Edro	Moretta	Ventre/Ventro
Fasciole	Muscatelli	Vermiglio
Fascioni	Pacelli	Volante

Family Stories

Councillor Flo Clucas (Valerio/Sanguinetti)

 My great, great, grandfather Stephan Sanguinetti was born in 1843 in Chiavari, Northern Italy and during the mid 19th century, he travelled to Buenos Aires and opened a leather business there. He later came to Bristol where he met Mary Ann Sweeney, who, at the time was working as a servant. They fell in love and planned to get married, the Sanguinetti's forebode the marriage and warned if Stephan went ahead with his intentions they would have nothing more to do with him. The marriage did go ahead regardless in 1863 and they had many children but unfortunately most died in infancy with only three children surviving, all girls named Lenora, Eugenie and Mary-Catherine. Mary-Catherine later married Celestino Valerio in 1883 at Holy Cross Church.

Celestino was born in Villa Latina (Aginone) and had been an artist's model whilst passing through various Italian cities. When he visited Florence on his journey northwards he was so taken by the city's charm, he named one of his daughters Florence. They set up their home a few doors down from the Sanguinetti's in Hunter Street and opened shops in both Hunter Street and Christian Street one selling fish & chips and the other selling rice pudding. They also had a large family; two of their sons, Anthony and Dominic Valerio were familiar boxers in Liverpool and trained at the local gym. A regular evening pursuit was to spend some time after their boxing session back at the family chip shop and retreat to the back room to play a few hands of cards with fellow boxers. On one occasion from the hallway came a terrific sound of crashing, the men all rushed to see what was causing the noise but to their utter astonishment the hallway was empty and unusually ice cold. The incident happened again on the following evening only this time uncle Tony was quick enough into the hallway to see a severed head come thumping down the stairs and vanish before reaching the bottom. Legend has it the house was once home to a seafarer and his wife and one night the seafarer came home unexpectedly and found his wife with another man, he fetched an axe and on the landing at the top of the stairs attacked the stranger, beheading him. I am unsure whether this story was told to scare us as children or it was actually true but the priest was called to the house to bless it on numerous occasions. My uncle Frank Valerio lived in London and was an international accordion player and often appeared at The London Palladium. Some Valerios actually made it to America and are listed on the Ellis Island list register. The Valerios made a good living from the shops and actually had their own servant called Elizabeth Sergeant who was later married to uncle Dominic.

The Christian Street chip shop was destroyed during the Blitz and so the Valerios moved up to 95 Brownlow Hill where my mother had a sweet shop next door. My mother would tell me how they would work through the blackouts as they often had 200 meal orders for the people in various shelters, a penny dinner consisted of sausage and chips and a two-penny dinner came with fish. On one evening they were caught up in a terrible air raid and had to stay in the shop until six o'clock the next morning. When they emerged they heard Lewis's had taken a direct hit and was still ablaze, they ventured up to see the devastation, all around, the city was filled with ash that resembled snow and amidst the burning embers they saw what was left of Lewis's. Liverpool is only now recovering from looking like a post war city, yet even today there are still signs of scars left by the Second World War.

Valerio chip shop, Christian Street.

Olive D'Annunzio and Daughter Lorraine

My grandparents were called Michele D'Annunzio and Fortunata Mancini and they were both born in a village called Atina in the hills of Lazio, Southern Italy. Like every other Italian traveller at that time they were escaping poverty that was just around the corner, so with all the money they had and their three children they came to Liverpool.

My father Felice Andrea was only nine at the time and thought it was a great adventure, it was the first time he had been on a ship. They found themselves in 55 Gerard Street and once they were settled in, Michele got work as a mosaic layer around the Brownlow Hill area of Liverpool. He was one of the most artistic, and often designed the layouts, his work was perfect and he was always in demand.

My father, Felice went to St Francis Xaviers School and married my mother Agnes Lang in Holy Cross Church. Her family owned a well-known shop in Hunter Street called Wally Langs. Later my parents lived in Whale Street and started their own small ice cream business. They used a yard in Back Bennett Street, which they shared with the Santangelli's.

My father was a very gifted man and could turn his hand to anything from cobbling shoes to making his own ice cream carts, but it was my mother who made the ice cream not him, and it was the most delicious taste you could ever imagine, they would take the carts all over Liverpool.

When I was two and a half my father died of bronchial problems, my mother, his brother Filipo (Puche) and sister Maria Grazia (Volante) were with him when he died. He left five sons and three daughters.

My father had planned to return to Italy with a fellow Italian called Romolo and had saved for a long time but Romolo made the journey alone neglecting to take my father, this angered my father and he died not long afterwards. He never got his wish to see his beloved village once more.

My mother's life took a downward turn and she was now faced with bringing up her children alone and carrying on with the family business, my uncle Filipo became my mother's saviour and helped out with the ice cream and accompanied her with the carts selling in the streets. It was hard work but my mother was determined she would provide for her children and they would grow up being a credit to their fathers memory.

When the war broke out the Italians suffered a lot my mother couldn't even go to New Brighton with her cart without having to go to Rose Hill Police Station first to inform them of her movements. Even though my mother was British she was shunned by neighbours because she had an Italian name, lots of Italians were anglicising their names at the time but my mother thought of how proud Felice was of his name and heritage so she put up with the malicious remarks rather than be called by anything else.

Agnes & Felice D'Annunzio.

Ray Baccino

My grandfather, Giovanni Baccino was born in Genoa, Northern Italy and during the late 19th century he came to Liverpool.

He quickly found accommodation in a boarding house owned by the Gianellis in Islington Place and started working for a local firm by the name of Diespeker. He undertook mosaic and terrazzo work at both St. Georges Hall and The Liver Buildings.

Life was extremely hard in them days, they had left Italy literally starving and walked the majority of the way finding work in whatever town they travelled through. My grandfather intended to go onto the States like the rest of his family but had run out of money and so settled here.

When the mosaic work in Liverpool dried up from time to time, my grandfather would pose for art students just to keep the roof above his head, or hire a hurdy gurdy and take it through the streets.

The war was a bad time for the Italians in the neighbourhood and one night the officials came to take my grandfather but to their total embarrassment and shock they were told he had died five years earlier.

My father Francis Baccino followed his father's footsteps and worked for Diespeker, after the war it was taken over by Conway Stefanutti. My father worked all over the country with fellow Italians, the Iellos, Minghellas and Gianellis, they would work six solid weeks and only then were they allowed a full weekend off. They worked wherever they were sent, one such place was Northern Ireland, my father was all set to go and at the last minute was told he was being sent to Scotland instead, so off he went up north. The man who took my father's place was actually killed in Northern Ireland for wearing a crucifix, something my father also wore.

I was born in Rose Gardens and went to Bishop Goss School. I can remember being sent like most other kids in the area to Jimmy Romeos (Imundi) in Springfield Street for various things, the beautiful smells inside the shop would send your hunger pangs racing. Another place I'd be sent if Jimmy Romeos was closed, was Coopers in Church Street where the tins of conserve were more posh because they had a whole bay leaf inside. One time Jimmy Romeo's shop was fire damaged and the woman who lived in number 1 Clare Street let her house be used as a makeshift shop. This was common among the Italian people they were very close and always helped each other.

I also went to work in the terrazzo trade and became a polisher, I did a lot of work in the old Royal Hospital, but one of the saddest things I have ever done was to dismantle the altar at St Joseph's Church in 1978. The church had been closed for a while, my mother was the last person to be buried from there in 1976, and one day I was walking past and glimpsed a team of men hacking away at the marble altar, I asked what they were doing and they told me they were taking it to pieces. I told them they were doing it all wrong so I was given the task of doing it myself and re-assembling it in Portobello Road, London, from there it was sold and went onto Saudi Arabia. It broke my heart to see the church like that, stripped of all the fantastic marble and statues.

As a child I remember the sounds of the buskers who would come into the tennies singing and playing the accordions and people would throw pennies over the landings. The weddings were always a big outdoor event, that's if the Italian mothers were finally persuaded to let their beloved sons get married. The people didn't want to leave Little Italy when it was getting pulled down but they were happy with Gerard Gardens as they were all put together and the new flats were like Buckingham Palace compared to the old neighbourhood.

Giovanni Baccino.

Baccino Family Portrait

Margaret Donnelly (nee Gildea) Holy Cross

I was born and raised in the Holy Cross area it was a unique place with a mix of Italian and Irish influences. On our landing in Fontenoy Gardens lived Freddy and Alice Innelli, they didn't have any children of their own and were so kind to the kids in the square and would often help pay for them to go on chara-bangs to Blackpool to see the lights. When I was chosen to be a trail bearer they paid for part of my outfit. At procession time every house in the parish was decorated, reams of paper would be bought many weeks before from money collected from the residents and turned into the most beautiful buntings and floral decorations you could imagine, each landing would have a certain colour and each occasion would have a dominant theme, for the crowning of Our Lady in May, the colours would be blue and white and for the Sacred Heart procession in June, the colours would be red and white. There was always a healthy rivalry between parishes and it never lost the excitement of who was going to be May Queen. The men in the parish would make the altar in front of the air raid shelter in the square and put up the trellis work for all the flowers to be attached. My brother Jimmy every year demanded he wouldn't be in the procession, because he was little he was always made to go in the front and my mam would say "you won't be in the front Jimmy I promise", and there he'd be with a right face on him in the front, half the flowers wouldn't have a head left on them because the lads would be messing around fighting beforehand. The people enhanced the parishes, regardless of their background they had one thing that brought them together and that was religion.

Christmas was always a lovely time in Fontenoy Gardens I can remember singing at midnight mass, all harmonising perfectly because we'd been practising since October. There would be an open crib and the church would be packed to the rafters, the bells would be ringing and all the kids wearing their new clothes giving everyone a twirl and showing off.

On the way home in the crisp night air the dispersing crowds would be shouting "all the best" to each other and drift off in different directions. Back home the fire would be banked up with loads of coal because it was Christmas and the flat would be filled with tantalising aromas of pork and turkey cooling in the kitchen. We would sit with a mug of cocoa in one hand, big meat butty in the other, with the lights off and the glow of the fire illuminating the room before going off to bed.

Whenever we were a bit flushed we got treated to a chip butty down at Chiappes on Scotland Road, there was always a load of lads and girls outside but there was never any trouble and you never felt scared or vulnerable. Every Sunday the older girls would be scrubbing the landings and the alleyo was swilled with the water, there was a lot of pride taken living in not just Fontenoy Gardens but all the tenements in the area. Everyone had the same background, we all bought off the Sturla's van, and we all had the same struggles but there was a sense of unity and care for one another. The kids playing in the square below didn't have one mother they had fifty looking over the landings watching out for them.

When Fontenoy got demolished in the 1980's and I went back for the last time to brush through, I looked out the window into the square and all them years came flooding back, the arch where the girls would play rounders and the square where the footy matches took place. As I closed the door for the last time I realised all them traditions had gone forever and would never return.

Holy Cross procession.

Rosa Ferrie and Family

My grandfather, Dominic Antonio Ferrie, boarded a ship in Naples at the end of the 19th century. He was heading for Bangor, Pennsylvania but with my grandfather not speaking very good English ended up in Bangor, North Wales. He stayed there for a while and married Ann Evans; they eventually came to Liverpool and lived at 25 Gerard Street. My grandfather found what work he could and had a number of occupations, the Italians were very hard workers and never idle. One of his many jobs was working on the Catholic Cathedral; he often said how he would come home exhausted but was just happy to be earning a wage.

My grandfather still owned property back in Italy that had been passed down through the family. In his later years he was befriended by two travelling Italians who said they knew the family back in Italy, on one occasion they took him out for a drink and whilst under the influence persuaded him to sell his Italian property, something he always regretted.

My father was also called Dominic Anthony Ferrie and he often reminisced about Little Italy and how the older Italians knew how to celebrate special events which often went on until the next day. On feast days there was always lots of preparation to do and each child would be given a job, every little detail was checked and checked again and then the whole family would walk through the streets in their best clothes to church.

The Italians were a very proud bunch, they never accepted charity but were more inclined to give it. Their religion was very important and going to church was a daily event and not an option.

In the neighbourhood there were many Italian bachelors living in the boarding houses, they often bought their meals from the local cookhouses, one of the favourites was situated in Soho Street, I can still remember the lovely smell of bread that came wafting through the streets.

My father was a soldier and was posted to many distant places such as India; he was even at The Battle of the Mons where he was terribly injured. After the war he worked for the railway at Edge Hill and every morning on his way to work he would call in to the St Mary of the Angels often making him late, but like most Italians this never seemed to phase my father who would always take everything in his stride.

We lived in William Henry Street and later I moved up to Rupert Hill with my own family and found work in St Francis Xaviers School and College as a cleaner.

I have a recipe for Macaroni that goes back to when my grandfather was a boy in Italy, the good food must have been the reason why the Italians lived long lives many of them well into their 90's as I am.

Rosa Ferrie

Ged Fagan, Gerard Gardens

 I can only see it as having been a privilege to grow up in Gerard Gardens. The colisseumesque arena created by the landings surrounding the square lent itself to a cracking football stadium, long before Munich built their Olympic attempt for 1972. The residents were the spectators. The matches, sometimes fifteen a side would go on there between the rival squares, usually it was twenty up, some games going on until dusk. As Lords or Wimbledon hit our Rediffusion push button tellies in the summer, so cricket wickets and tennis courts would be chalked out and girls would play hopscotch or gutters. Another of their pastimes was for a skipping rope to be held at each end as they 'called their mates into the middle' first one then two, then three. It was a vibrant happy place, seldom empty until you were eventually called in one by one for your tea and then back down there again.

Living so close to town and William Brown Street in particular, the statues in St. Johns Gardens made brilliant hiding places for mega long hide 'n' seek games, that is until the cocky watchman came out of his hut under the stairs to chase you away. We often played off ground tick around the Walker Art Gallery walls or generally messing about on the Wellington Column or in the Steble fountain. The Museum was a weekend must for following girls around from floor to floor, did we ever say anything to any of them though?

Come the end of October and the old bombdie warehouses of Islington would supply the bonfire wood for yet another year as kids traipsed back to base, hidden beneath the doors that they carried. The loot would have to be stored securely from the thieving neighbouring squares, usually on the tenement roofs. And so to the night itself and praying the rain would hold off, it never seemed to. Flames reaching above the 3rd landing by seven o'clock, but you would tell your mate from another square in school next day that they were reaching above the roof, but so were his. You would hear fire engines racing up Scotland Road or along St. Anne Street, somebody's fun cut short. Smouldering bedsprings and pram frames a few hours later with the last of the kids poking the fire to keep it going, a lost cause. Next day, that football pitch I mentioned earlier would be a circle of melted tar.

Gerard Gardens archway.

Hilary Giannasi

Both of my grandparents were Italian, my grandmother; Martha Gestra married Luigi Giannasi, who was born in Lucca, Northern Italy. He came here to Liverpool in 1861 and was a very talented craftsman, he made plaster figurino statues. One of his best friends was old Mr Gianelli who my grandfather actually travelled with from Italy.

My grandfather had a very popular shop with fellow Italian Frediani and an Irishman called Regan; they made wonderful intricate religious statues for the local churches and neighbourhood usually of popular Saints amongst the Italian and Irish community. The statues were then painted in great detail and almost looked life like.

My uncle Angelo became the oldest altar boy at Sacred Heart every morning he would prepare the altar ready for the mass later on, he would make breakfast for everyone and only then would he go to his own job.

I was born in Vauxhall Gardens, Highfield Street and spent most of my youth in the streets of Little Italy; I went to Holy Cross School and then won a scholarship to Walton Technical Collage, later working in Dickson's Stationers. I can remember how proud my mother was when I won the scholarship and she made sure all the neighbours knew about it.

Hunter Street was full of tiny shops all selling different wares, you never had to go to town even though it was on your doorstep everything you needed could be bought in them streets. They were never empty from morning until night and the mix of different accents and languages all in one place was incredible to hear.

When the war came my family were evacuated to St Teresa's Parish in Norris Green, my father Louis was in the army and the rumours that went around telling of how when the Italian men enlisted they were being taken to interment camps was enough to scare half of the families to death.

My father was sent to Belgium and he hadn't seen his brother Angelo for a very long time, one day he heard someone shouting his name from the middle of nowhere he turned to find it was Angelo, he was so relieved as he had began to give up hope of ever seeing him again.

It is very sad that there isn't any Little Italy as such anymore, there are still lots of Italian families living in the area and the stories are being lost over time.

Giannasi, Regan & Frediani.

Nick Riozzi

The Riozzi family left Picinisco, Southern Italy in 1887 and travelled northwards towards France; the family consisted of my great grandparents, Francesco and Maria, my grandparents Pasquale and Angelina and their children.

When they arrived in Liverpool they had every intention of carrying on to America but word was going around that the Italians were getting a poor reception in the southern states with low wages and shoddy living conditions. So like many other Italians they decided to stay in Liverpool and settled in a lodging house in Clare Street.

Before my grandfather Pasquale came to Italy he had been to London years earlier and posed as an artist's model, apparently T.H Laurence was travelling around the Comino Valley and spotted him and saw his potential.

My grandfather made his own ice cream carts and barrel organs and hired them out to the Italians in the neighbourhood. One of the reasons Little Italy was located on the edge of town was the theatres were close by and this was a good source of income for the street entertainers.

My father Anthony was born in Liverpool and served as an Army Officer in the First World War he was terribly wounded in France and my mother travelled there to be with him. He later went to Northern Italy and acted as an interpreter while he was there he met Ernest Hemmingway, my father was awarded the Military Cross.

I went to St Francis Xavier's School and I excelled at art and was asked to draw the stained glass windows of S.F.X Church for its centenary, the drawings ended up in the Walker Art Gallery as 'The Schoolboys Exhibition'. Living within the Italian neighbourhood was fine but whenever I went into other areas I was always getting ambushed for being Italian and often came home with cuts and bruises. It was tough growing up in them days but it made us what we are today.

Anthony & Mary Riozzi with Bridget & Joseph.

The Minghellas

Our grandparents were Giacomo Minghella and Domenica Riozzi, they had a son Francis who was born in 1893 in Italy and within the following four years they had arrived in Liverpool and had a second son Philip in 1897. They lived in Gerard Street where they had a further two sons, our father Antonio born in 1899 and Dominic born in 1907.

Giacomo was a street musician and they were first registered in the 1901 census. Due to their inability to speak English our name has taken on many different variations such as Minchella, munghella and muncelli.

Like most other Italians we have connections with the Inelli and Colletta families, whilst living in Little Italy our father Anthony went to Holy Cross School and played for the boys football team, he often remarked how after the match most of the lads would pawn their footy boots in Berry's pawn shop until the next match day.

He met and married our mother, Catherine Cooke in 1925 and had sixteen children in all, some died in infancy, one of our brothers Anthony was killed in a traffic accident on London Road when he was two. Our family didn't stay in Little Italy and moved extensively throughout Liverpool. Our father joined the Royal Navy at a very young age and fought in the war, this didn't stop an angry mob threaten to smash our windows because we were Italian though. Our grandmother Domenica couldn't speak a word of English and we had to hide her at stages throughout the war, she was terrified of being interned.

After the war our father found employment with a company called Diespeker, who specialised in terrazzo and mosaic work. He did extensive work at the Town Hall during the 1950s and 1960s, the staircase in Littlewoods, Church Street and the Royal Hospital. In his spare time he created beautiful mosaic steps in all our houses.

We feel we know little of our family history back in Italy but it has never stopped us being proud of our heritage and what stories we do have we make sure they have been handed down to our children and grandchildren who have all shown a genuine interest.

Antonio in the Royal Navy.   *Antonio & Catherine Minghella's wedding.*

Tony Judge (Ventre)

I was born in number 7 Lionel Street and my mother was Madalena Ventre and as you can imagine whilst living in the heart of Little Italy music was being played all the time. My mother was an accomplished violinist, my grandfather played the harp, my grandmother played the mandolin, my uncle Tony was a very gifted tenor and my uncle John played the violin on stage. With all this talent music was not a past time but a way of making money. My father was a seafarer and he would always bring home copies of the latest music from New York, and as you can imagine this made him a very popular man in the neighbourhood. My grandfather along with some of his family and friends played onboard the Pier Head to Eastham Ferry for many years. My love of music stems from the age of seven when my uncle Tony gave me my first lesson on the harp and I was hooked from then on. When all the streets and houses in Little Italy were being demolished for Gerard Gardens my grandmother was moved out to Dovecot and my music lessons came to an end until when the war started and the bombing became heavy I was asked to go and live with my 'Nin' for company. It was then she introduced me to the mandolin and we would spend many happy hours playing duets. When she died I inherited her mandolin and it is my most cherished possession. I eventually joined a mandolin orchestra in 1960 and although the numbers have dwindled over the years we are still going strong and are called The Wirral Mandoliers.

The Wirral Mandoliers.

Stella Muller (Volante)

By 1907 Guston (Gaetano)Volante and his wife Marie Antoinette owned a boarding house at 82 Gerard Street, they often had seasonal workers boarding there such as basket-weavers and shoemakers who came from Italy to sell their wares in the summer months.

Their son, Raphael was a 'jack of all trades' and was married to Mary Guatelli, they also lived at number 82. Mary, although Italian by birth, cooked and prepared the most authentic Irish dishes in her own basement cookhouse, spare ribs and cabbage, Irish stew and bread & butter pudding to name but a few were very popular around the neighbourhood.

A long awaited child for Raphael and Mary came in the form of Madeline Volante (my mother) and was christened in Holy Cross, but happiness was short lived when four years later Mary died leaving little Madeline without a mother. Her father married a few years later, he and his wife Margaret Murphy lived nearby and went on to have four more children.

Madeline continued to live with her grandparents at number 82 Gerard Street and attended Holy Cross School. She especially liked to see the Italian jewellery men coming around the neighbourhood and was never without plenty of jewellery bought by her doting grandparents. Every year she and her grandparents returned to Italy and brought back to Liverpool plenty of sausages, cheeses and preserves for the coming year.

In the basement stood big ovens that were used as kilns for the boarders who sculptured the figurines of the Italian Saints and sold them around the streets.

One of the large parlours at number 82 was rented out for card games and many Jewish businessmen reserved it for their Sabbath, the stakes were often very high and some of the men gambled away their entire businesses at that table. But all was not lost as Madeline and her cousins would lie in wait for the game to end and search the room floor in the hope of finding the odd lost shilling or two.

There were many large processions through the tiny streets of Little Italy, the Volantes would be dressed in their best clothes and Madeline would walk in the procession carrying a beautiful painting of her mother in her traditional dress.

Every Easter Sunday her grandmother would prepare a traditional dish of salted fish in batter for their breakfast, the dish had been eaten on that day from when her grandmother was a child back in Atina, Italy.

Madeline's grandfather was a good storyteller and would have the children enthralled with stories of how when he was a young man he walked from Southern Italy to the Swiss border before he boarded a ship to Liverpool and later he sent for his wife and children.

On one occasion her grandfather and father Raphael went to watch a friend box at the Adelphi Theatre Tavern in Circus Street. The friend was being beaten so badly that her grandfather raced home to fetch two huge swords from his parlour to kill the man who was beating his friend, the police were called to prevent him from going back inside the theatre and he was barred for the rest of his life.

The summer Madeline left school, Lena Macari from Bristol visited; Lena was Madeline's relative. The Macaris had an ice cream business in Bristol, and they needed someone to take care of their disabled son Johnny. So Madeline went off to live with the Macaris and took care of their children. The Macari's were also in the music and entertaining business and were known as The Dutch Serenades, Billy Merry who sang with the band later became Madeline's husband. They married in September 1933 and I was born in June 1934. We were living in London during the war and were bombed out of our homes several times, we ended up living with my great, grandfather Volante who by this time had left Liverpool and was living in South Shields. Whilst living there we endured the worst night of the war when the sirens sounded we quickly made our way to the shelter in the garden my mother took my newly born sister out of the pram and left the pram outside as it wouldn't fit through the door, a bomb struck the house sending glass flying, when they came out of the shelter there in the pram was a huge piece of glass where the baby had just been lying. We later were evacuated to Ovingham near Scotland, my sister and I attended school there, after nearly a year we finally set up home in Clacton-On-Sea where we stayed for many years. After divorcing my father in 1946 my mother took on several jobs and ended up working in the hotel industry she would work long hard hours sometimes starting at six in the morning and not returning home until midnight. My mother finally retired in 1969.

Madeline, Marie and Guston Volante.

The Dutch Serenades at The Palladium.

Uncle Ralph Volante playing Macbeth.

Paul Sudbury The Fall of Gerard Gardens

The location of Gerard Gardens had always made it susceptible to the many road developments in the city centre. The Churchill flyovers in the late 1960s resulted in a 'floating motorway' running parallel with Hunter Street. A major ring road surrounding the tenement blocks was planned in the 1970s, but was scrapped following campaigns by the Vauxhall Neighbourhood Council. The 1980s finally led to the demise of the flagship-housing scheme, with lack of investment and maintenance by various councils leaving Gerard Gardens with a sorry look on its face. A scheme to widen Hunter Street dictated that the tenements would be demolished.

Sloan Doyle carried out the demolition in stages, with a section of Gerard Crescent being the first to fall. My mam lived in 4b, and was moved to a vacant flat further along the landing whilst demolition took place. Astonishingly she was moved again to another vacant flat on the block on Christian Street (known locally as the Holy Block); she was the only person living in that block at the time. Eventually a new house was built in the St Joseph's Crescent area, a 2 bed semi with front and back garden. However, she never settled in the new house, and harked back to the days of standing out on the landing and talking to passing neighbours. A number of the council tenants lived in appalling conditions during the migration to the new houses, with armies of rats being flushed out by the demolition. In fifty short years Gerard Gardens had gone from one man's vision of utopia for the masses, to a dilapidated demolition site.

I think that its death was premature; many residents did not want to leave. Ex resident Tony Vaughan remarked that when the blocks were demolished, he felt as though a piece of him had died.

Gerard Gardens was much more than bricks and mortar, it was built on the foundations of communities from the Little Italy area of Liverpool.

People who realised that happiness came, not from getting what you want, but by wanting what you already have. I remember the close social network that existed in times of crisis, in particular the three day week in the early 1970s.With the housewives all pulling together to make the best of low incomes as a result of their husband's reduced working hours.

All the houses had coal fires at the time, and we would sit for hours in the blackouts playing cards by the flickering flames. When I started work people would ask where I lived, when I told them it was Gerard Gardens they would take a step back in fear. To many their only exposure to the block was passing it on the L3 to Crosby, and seeing a gang of kids playing under the arch. They felt pity that people had to live there, but they were on the outside looking in. I never realised that we were poor, and never felt that my life was lacking any material possessions (though I always wanted Mousetrap!), because I was always surrounded by family and friends. We had the freedom to roam and play, and money doesn't necessarily buy you that.

Paul & Daughter when demolition began.

The Boner family

 My grandfather Mark Boner left the Picinisco area of Italy and came to Liverpool at the age of seventeen along with his brother and sister, towards the late 1800's. He met and married Angelina Granelli and lived in a court off Scotland Road, they had three children John, Louis and Christina. Mark, accompanied by a small bear would travel the country, join goose fairs, and entertain the crowds. He returned to Italy leaving my grandmother with three small children, after seven years she had him declared dead so she could re-marry and went on to have four daughters. My father John Boner and my mother Margaret O'Shaughnessy were married in Holy Cross Church and set up home in Gerard Street, my father was a prominent man in the community and led several church groups such as, The Young Men's Society and helped organise the religious processions that took place during the summer. He made religious artefacts such as portable communion boxes that were taken into the homes of the sick in the parish. He made the most beautiful wooden toys for his sixteen children and many grandchildren. My father fought in the Boer War and the First World War and during the Second World War he was an air raid patrolman. Our house in Gerard Street was converted into a grocery shop and cookhouse selling scouse, rice pudding and roasts. Whenever the Grand National took place and the countless Irish dignitaries made their way to stay at the Adelphi Hotel the manager would send an order to the cookhouse for pig's feet and cabbage to serve his guests. When Gerard Street was making way for the gardens we moved to the Bull Ring along with many other Italian families. My father lived until he was 100 but sadly, he passed away the same day at the exact time he was born ten minutes to midnight.

A day out in Little Italy.

Andrew Smith

As a child I grew up hearing the fabulous stories of my late grandfather, Johnny Holleran, many of these stories revolved around the colourful life of a man named Dom Volante. A man at that time I only knew as the man with the fancy boxed cakes.

Dom would often visit my grandfather, as he was married to Dom's niece, Marie Coletta daughter of Luigi Coletta and Madalena Volante, and, he would always, to my delight, bring boxes containing the best cream cakes tied decoratively with string.

As I grew older I would go to watch boxing tournaments held at the Grafton with my grandfather and again would hear more tales of Dom's life on our way home. My grandfather had collected an archive of newspaper cuttings spanning Dom's boxing career that he would always refer to. However sometime after Dom's passing this archive was lent in good faith to a reporter who wanted to write an article on Dom's life to our families dismay they were never returned!

Fast forward a decade or so and I had taken an interest in filmmaking and made a short documentary. My proposal was to make a piece on the great Dom Volante, the Liverpool fighting machine, the company literally bit my hand off and told me that they would be happy to support me in making a documentary about Dom.

Unfortunately, my grandfather had passed on by this time but his stories remained and I took to the boxing clubs and pubs to do my research. To my amazement ninety percent of people I spoke to had a story to tell about Dom or could put me in the direction of people that could.

I received a great deal of support from many communities and organisations namely the Merseyside Ex Boxers Association and the Scottie Press. Once complete the film was received very well and continues to do so, which I believe is a great testament to Dom's great ability and character.

For me it has been an amazing journey in terms of the people I have met and relatives I was not even aware of, it has played a small but important part in reuniting distant relatives and the wider Liverpool-Italian community as will this book. Finally one last word, during my research I had lots of strokes of luck but without doubt the biggest had to be the reclaiming of my grandfather's archive of newspaper clippings which are now back in their rightful home.

Dom Volante.

The Riozzi Family

Our family originate from the Picinisco area of Italy, in 1887 the family settled in Liverpool's Little Italy and had numerous businesses there. Our grandparents Angelina and Pasqual Riozzi made their own ice cream and as children we often accompanied Pasqual to the freezing house in Fraser Street and helped with making the ice cream and of course eating it. In 1928 our grandfather was killed on Christian Street by a tram, leaving our grandmother with several children to rear up on her own. Our father Francis was born in Liverpool and went to Saint Francis Xaviers School and when he left he became a highly skilled terrazzo and mosaic polisher.

His technique was a very well kept secret ensuring he was always in demand, he did repair work to St Georges Hall and St Anthony's altar. At one time during the 1950's he was flown out to the Hebrides to do restoration work on a church there. Our father would come home from work with his hands torn and bleeding in complete agony but he never moaned about the pain and was always ready for the next job. He met and married our mother Bridget Higgins and they had ten children, we moved a lot during our childhood but whilst we lived in Clare Street and Marshall Terrace we attended local schools and just before the war we went to the Italian School. Our teacher was Miss Salvadora; the school held the most fantastic parties at Reece's Café in town where we were given more toys than we could carry. We were taught to count in Italian and so on, however our schooling was brought to an abrupt end when our parents found out the songs we were encouraged to sing and that we were saluting Mussolini at the end of the class. We were only young children and didn't realise the true significance of the school, we were just happy with the toys and parties.

The families had such pride in their homes and were constantly cleaning them. Although the families were huge they were well cared for and the Italians were far from work shy. Italian fathers made very good fathers and were very loving people. Some of the Italian families still spoke their own language and encouraged their children to do the same. A treat for us was to go to Capaldi's sweet shop in Springfield Street, but first we had our chores to do, one of our jobs we were given as children was scrubbing our front step, we were always very proud of it as our father had made it from mosaic as well as a fantastic terrazzo kitchen floor. Our brother Vincent followed our fathers footsteps and worked for St James Tiles in Liverpool, after our father died Vincent went to live in America where he still has a business called Riozzi Marble and Tile .

Francis and Bridget Riozzi with their ten children.

Jim Dunn Retired Parish Priest (St Joseph's)

Bishop Goss School was named after the former Bishop of Liverpool who had distinguished himself as a promoter of education. Originally the school comprised of one building now known as Victoria Building and housed the infants, juniors and seniors together. Eventually the seniors were housed in a new building in the 1920s. The school had a rooftop playground and an extensive assembly hall in the basement. In the 1970s a new dining room/gymnasium wing was added as well as an administration block.

My mum died when I was two and so my aunty brought me up, she was a cleaner at the District Bank in Great Homer Street, before leaving for work my aunty would get my breakfast ready and off she would go leaving me to make my own way to school, which was only a short distance. On my way each morning I would stop someone, usually a gentleman, and ask... "Hey Mister would you tie my laces?" Once I arrived the Headmistress, Sister Gerard would allow me to sit by the coal fire to get warm before school began. Once when the schools religious inspector came he asked, "How long do souls stay in purgatory?" to which I answered "forever Father" My teacher, Miss Brockbank was not pleased with me I can tell you. Another teacher, Mr Murphy, who lived in Everton Brow, was so affected by the poverty of some of the school children he bought one child a pair of shoes. The children from the worse off families were provided for by the police charity. Boys were given thick corduroy pants and clogs to wear.

The parish held colourful processions on the 17th of March for St Patrick's Day and on the 12th of July marking the anniversary of The Battle of the Boyne. In 1937 just before the Second World War, Parish Priest Father Green celebrated his Silver Jubilee. The parish held a magnificent procession in Gerard Gardens and other surrounding tenements, the balconies were festooned with buntings, the kerbstones were whitewashed and the windows were decorated with beautiful hand made paper flowers.

Greetings were painted on the walls "God bless Father Green" and strings of flags hung across the streets. The crowds gathered and amongst them were The Children of Mary, The Young Men's Society and The Union of Catholic Mothers. Father Green joined the procession in a car provided by the local undertaker, people cheered, waved and shouted "God bless Father Green" as he passed.

The processions usually ended up with the people of St Joseph's migrating to the local pub for light refreshments! Just to confirm that it had all been worth it and they had done the parish proud. The families of the parish had little money and life was hard with constant trips to the washhouse and lugging heavy bags from Great Homer Street, so a procession gave them something to look forward to and the next best thing to a holiday.

During the Second World War in 1941 the school wing was destroyed by a land mine and many children were being evacuated, most returned after a short time but instead of being taught at the school they were distributed around the area. I was in a group that met at Lawrence Gardens; the flat was on the first floor and belonged to Mrs O'Donnell who had a grocery shop at the top of the street, but time was limited and the families who provided the accommodation had to get on with their own lives, so lessons were kept short.

I returned to St Joseph's in 1976 as Parish Priest and Chairman of Governors. There was an air of despondency about the school. The Head, Mr Costigan, was convinced the new Archbishop (Derek Worlock) would close the parish down. The church was full of dry rot and the number of pupils at the school had fallen. A decision was made to demolish the church, however the school and a small chapel remained for a further twenty years.

Father Green's Jubilee procession 1937.

Mary Madeline Fennell (Frediani & Gianelli Family)

 My grandfather, Guiseppi Frediani, came to Liverpool in the middle of the 19th century and was one of the first Italians to settle here in the Christian Street area. The Frediani family have always been linked to crafting the plaster religious figures for local churches, this was a profession that they were legendary for back in Northern Italy and although I am not absolutely sure I believe the shop was situated on Hunter Street.

Guiseppi met and married my grandmother, Catarina Gianelli and from what I can gather this is were the famous chip shop emporium began. My grandmother owned two chip shops, the first was located on Cazneau Street and another on Scotland Road, and although I am slightly biased, my grandmother made the best chips in Liverpool!

A well known joke around Liverpool was how the 'Germans bombed our chippys during the war', unfortunately in the Frediani's case this was true, during the Second World War a land mine fell near the shop but didn't explode, we were evacuated and thought we'd had a narrow escape, however the following night the shop was bombed and totally ruined. This is the main reason I do not have many pre-war photographs or family artefacts.

I can remember the Gianelli's chip shop on Christian Street very well, Maria and her two brothers Frank and Johnny were legends behind the counter, they were well respected in the Little Italy area and took part in numerous community ventures. Frank Gianelli received The Bene Merenti Medal for exceptional service to the Catholic Church. Their shop was mid way between two theatres and so was very popular amongst the famous actors that played there.

When I was a child I attended the Italian School along with my best friend Josie Pacelli who lived in Lambeth Street, her family had a cookhouse there and sold mouth-watering meals such as boiled beef and roast potatoes, the aromas from the shop were unbelievable. Josie was one of the pupils that showed great talent at the Italian School and was taken to Italy as part of the reward for learning the language so well, it was believed that whilst in Italy, unaware, they put on a show and danced before Mussolini. Josie later joined The Women's Army and became a policewoman.

My aunty Maddie had a lodging house in Christian Street and housed seasonal workers from Italy. During the internment the workers were actually taken from the premises and sent to the Isle of Man, although it was not as bad as being sent to Canada onboard The Arandora Star. My uncle John Frediani joined The King's Royal Rifle Core and at El Alamein on 24th of October 1942, he was killed age 32, he had been a pupil at St Francis Xaviers and is listed on a plaque there in remembrance to those who lost their lives fighting for their country.

John Frediani.

The Smith (Volante/Colletta) family

Our great grandparents were Maria Grazia D'Annunzio and Vincenzo Volante and our grandparents were Madeline Volante and Louis Colletta, we are also related to the Minghellas.

When our grandfather Louis Colletta was told his daughter Winnie wouldn't live, he asked God to save the baby and in appreciation he declared he would walk to St Winifred's Well in Holywell bare footed, word got around Little Italy and he was supported by everyone in both St Joseph's and Holy Cross parishes. He made the journey and his daughter Winnie lived into her thirties. This goes to prove what the Italian families were like; they were determined, strong willed and generous people who often went out of their way to help others less fortunate.

Our families lived in both Christian Street and Gerard Street and our 'Nin' was the first resident in Gerard Gardens. When the Second World War started our grandfather Louis Colletta had to move out of Liverpool because the officials said he was an 'alien', by this they meant he didn't have a British passport. We went to live in Wigan with other relatives for fear if we stayed in Little Italy, Louis would be interned, the whole family eventually moved out there and some of us were born in Wigan. Our Father John Holleren had to make the journey to Camell Lairds every morning. Another member of the family, Philip Minghella was actually interned but was later rescued by a Liverpool Tory candidate and although the rest of the family were staunch Labour supporters aunty Lizzie voted Tory from then on!

We often went to visit our great grandmother, Maria Grazia Volante who by then was bed-ridden and taken care of by her daughter Leah who had a thing for cleaning. This was common amongst the Italians as they always kept their homes in pristine condition. Uncle Dom was cruising the Atlantic onboard the Cunard Liners, there was always an abundance of Philadelphia cheese brought back by him long before it was readily available in the shops.

Andrew Smith has recently paid tribute to his great uncle Dominic Volante in the form of a dvd documenting his amazing boxing career.

Whenever our uncle Dom visited our mum she would always send him home on the bus to Huyton with a huge bowl full of macaroni. Uncle Dom thought it was hysterical when the bus would be filled with the tantalizing aroma of our mum's cooking and he could hear the passenger's stomachs starting to rumble. We are all so very proud of our ancestry and ensure the stories are carried on for future generations.

Pat Holleren & Jimmy Lavin's wedding
(Winnie 1st row 2nd right)..

Julia Moore, St Joseph's girl

 My family consisted of my four sisters and five brothers all living with my parents in number 15 Peover Street in Little Italy. I can remember everyone being excited when Gerard Gardens was built and we moved to number 9a, we had for the first time an indoor toilet and hot running water, the things people take for granted nowadays.

I went to school with many Italian kids and two of my sisters married Italian lads Tony D'Annunzio and Robert Labio.

I went to St Joseph's School and then onto the Bishop Goss Seniors and we had to go to church every morning. Being a bit of a rebellious child I remember joining other kids and hiding in Comus Street and pretending to go until the eagle eyed Sister Gerard and Sister Agnes found out, I got a right pasting off my mam.

The processions were always a big event in the neighbourhood, my dad, Billy Wyles and my brother Stevie often carried the statues through the streets and I would walk in the procession in my improvised communion dress. It was a case of 'make do and mend' as we were still living with rationing and clothing coupons at the time, yet the people of St Joseph's turned out the most fantastic processions. There was a lot of rivalry between the neighbouring parishes and the kids often got into squabbles stating "our procession was better than yours!"

In Gerard Gardens we had our own playground but as we got older we played around the William Brown Street and St Georges Hall area away from the hundreds of eyes peering over the landings waiting to tell your mam what you had been up to and me being in The Guild of St Agnes had to keep up appearances.

My mam Josephine (nee Cowley) was one of the people who was called on to 'lay out' the dead of the parish, she would turn a room of the deceased's house into a beautiful grotto filled with candles, flowers, ribbons and smilax, this seems to be a lost art nowadays.

One of the biggest events that took place in Gerard Gardens was the filming of The Violent Playground. The kids were buzzing around like flies for days, although the older people were not impressed in the least when the Director replaced their pristine washing hanging out over the landings with rags that were only fit for the bin, in order to give the impression the people were living in poverty and filth.

When the final decision was made to demolish Gerard Gardens I couldn't bare to see it get knocked down, although I had left after I was married years beforehand it was still my home. The tenements had a future and they should have been given the chance to prove it as in the case of the Bullring, which is still going strong.

Tommy O'Keefe and Stevie Wyles at a
St Joseph's procession.

Brian McDonald

John Granelli was a farm labourer in Santa Maria Del Taro near the province of Genoa, Northern Italy. In the early 1850s he and at least one other brother left their village and headed for the 'new world' by foot. By the middle of the 1850s they had arrived in Manchester, whilst John's brother set up a lucrative ice cream business John, met and married Jane O'Riley and both came to Liverpool and settled in number 6 Lionel Street.

This to my knowledge makes John one of the earliest immigrants in Liverpool. They had four children...Jane who married Mario Boner, Mary-Madalena and Christine who married Anselmo and Antonio Ventre and John who married Elizabeth McDonald. John Granelli tried his hand in the ice cream trade making him the first to do so in Liverpool however, he was not as successful as his brother in Manchester largely due to him liking a pint or two and whilst out plying his trade in Seaforth Sands from a horse drawn cart he would make one too many stops for light refreshments and end up falling asleep on the way home leaving the horse to make his own way home to the stables in Lionel Street.

My father, John Granelli Jnr was born in Lionel Street in 1922 a year before the bulldozers moved in making him one of the last children to be born in the old Little Italy. The family then moved out to Dovecot and the name was then anglicised to Granell this still did not deter racism and prejudice in the new estates and so my father changed his name to McDonald (mother's maiden name) to help fit into their new life outside of the old community.

My father was twice severely wounding during the Sicily landings of the Second World War and received the last rites on both occasions. He was nursed back to health by his mother and a wonderful lady Mary Hornby (nee Ventre), undoubtedly if my father had not changed his name he would have been interned.

When my family lived opposite the Ventres in Lionel Street they were the closest of neighbours, friends and united in marriage, sadly most of these wonderful people I knew as a child have gone, which emphasises the importance of books like Terry Cooke's Little Italy and Debra D'Annunzio's Liverpool's Italian families it is excellent that their memories can live on.

John Granelli (McDonald)
with son John Jnr.

Anthony Vermiglio and sons

Dominic Vermiglio arrived in Liverpool from Chiavre, Northern Italy in 1892 and settled around the Scotland Road area. I grew up in William Henry Street and my family's trade was fish and chips and ice cream parlours. The family owned several shops in the Soho Street and Springfield Street area. One of my grandfather's traditions was preparing our Sunday breakfast of macaroni and bringing it through the streets to our house, I think I only got to see him on a Sunday so I always waited patiently for him on the doorstep. Boxing was a big thing in the Vermiglio household and several of them went to the Friary gym some even went on to train the youngsters from the area. During the Second World War whilst in Egypt, Albert and Joe Vermiglio boxed for the Army in front of Winston Churchill. Tom Vermiglio enlisted in the Royal Air Force and was shot down over Germany on the first day of the war; he had been a teacher at the Friary.

Our family suffered during the internment, the windows of the family chip shop were smashed and they were threatened by a mob that had congregated outside, but the family fronted the mob and having been boxers sent them packing. Regardless of this, the family were harassed throughout the war and at one stage changed the name to Verman.

The Vermiglio's are related to the Muscatelli's who also suffered during the war and some of their family were interned. I always remember one of the older members of the Muscatellis lived in the Four Squares and had a fantastic mosaic front step, someone reported him to the council who came around and ordered him to take it up, when he asked why? The council said "well nobody else has one" so Mr Muscatelli offered to do steps for everyone, unfortunately the council refused and poor Mr Muscatelli's mosaic step was removed.

Albert and Joseph

Dom (The Little Atom)

Conclusion

The history of Liverpool's Little Italy has extended more than 150 years and within this period a community of exceptional people evolved. The Italians created a diverse network that constantly adapted to new ways of life in order to survive; yet they still kept their own customs and traditions close at heart which made them unique.

Episodes of contention and discrimination especially during the mass migration and war years resulted in the people creating even stronger bonds with fellow Italians within their community. Determination and hard work was paramount in providing a better life for themselves and their children.

It has been said that the locality of Liverpool's Little Italy was one of the harshest, poverty stricken and unhealthiest places to live, however the intention of this book was to prove otherwise. The area provided churches, schools, shops, entertainment and homes albeit modest, for decent, industrious and respectable people.

With the so called slum clearance of many homes and small shops making way for luxurious tenement housing the Italian families were faced with rebuilding their empires, they continued to serve the community and integrated into British society, however the sacrifices the older Italians made should never be forgotten. To risk everything you have and embark upon a journey unaware of what the future held took great courage and confidence.

I have yet to find a person of Italian descent who is not interested in their heritage, they remain passionate about their family history even when so much has been lost through time.

Although the vibrant and colourful neighbourhood of Little Italy has dispersed with regeneration thankfully the fond stories carry on in present day Anglo/Italian families and it is to them I wish to propose my sincere gratitude and devote this book to Liverpool's Italian families.

Goodbye Scottie Road

The years have past since my last abode,
was Dryden Street in old Scottie Road.
Times have changed since I was there,
No Chiappe's cafe, no Vicky Square.

There's no Rotunda, no Champion Whates,
No Paddy's market, no Mary Kates
The Gaiety's gone, the Derby too,
And those Mary Ellen's are very few.

Even the scuffer on the beat,
no longer walks the lonely street.
Once there were people with smiling faces,
now there's nothing but dust and empty spaces.

Now Sunday football was played in the street,
and salt-fish for breakfast was quite a treat.
We had fresh necks, spare-ribs and thick barley soup,
and pans full of scouse what the old girl cooked.

There was the Washhouse were women fought for a mangle,
and after the fight they would have a good jangle.
There was the Morning Star pub where the Irishmen lurked,
while over a pint they'd talk about work.

Now here's some famous boxers who to watch was a joy.
Volante, Gannon, Butcher, Tommy and Jimmy Molloy.
And here's some famous soccer stars I must give credit too,
Morrisey, Tansey, Melia, Campbell and the Gannon's two.

Yes, these are only memories now of my last abode,
memories of my younger days in good old Scottie Road.
So it's "Goodbye Scottie Road!" old friend we'll never meet again,
for even though you're being rebuilt you'll never be the same!

By Terry Baines 1970